You Are the Eyes of the World

Wake up to find out that
you are the eyes of the world,
Wake now, discover that you are the song
that the morn-in' brings.

You Are the
Eyes of the World

Longchenpa

Translated by

Kennard Lipman and Merrill Peterson

under the inspiration of

Namkhai Norbu

Snow Lion Publications
Ithaca, NY   USA

Snow Lion Publications
P.O. Box 6483
Ithaca, New York 14851 USA
(607) 273-8519
www.snowlionpub.com

Printed in the USA on acid-free, recycled paper.

ISBN 978-1-55939-367-6

THIS BOOK BELONGS TO THE COPPER MOUNTAIN SERIES.

The Library of Congress cataloged the previous edition of this work as follows:
    Kloṅ-chen-pa Dri-med- 'od-zer, 1308-1363.
        [Byaṅ chub kyi sems kun byed rgyal po'i don khrid rin chen sgru bo.
English]
        You are the eyes of the world. / Longchenpa ; translated by Ken-
    nard Lipman and Merrill Peterson under the inspiration of Namkhai
    Norbu.
                        p.   cm.
        Includes bibliographical references and index.
        ISBN 1-55939-140-5
        1. Tripiṭaka. Sūtrapiṭaka. Tantra. Sarvadharmamahāśāntibodhicitta-
    kulayarāja.—Introductions—Early works to 1800. 2. Rdzogs-chen (Rñiṅ-
    ma-pa) I. Lipman, Kennard. II. Peterson, Merrill, 1949- . III. Title.

        BQ 2180.S255 K5813 2000
        294.3'85—dc21   00-026529

for everyone

Contents

Preface   xi

Textual Introduction   1
    The *kun byed rgyal po*   1
    Sutra, Tantra, and Agama   2
    Longchenpa's Guide   7

Introduction   11
    The Spiritual Quest   11
    Overview of the Text   13
    How to Read the Text   16

The Jewel Ship   17
    Anthem   19
    Preface   19
    Introduction   20
    List of Subjects   23
        I. The Spiritual Advisor   24
        II. The Student   25
        III. The Teaching   26
            A. The Spiritual Heritage   27

B. The Main Subject Matter   29
   1. Guruyoga   29
     The Visualization and Guruyoga   29
   2. The Real Subject Matter   31
     a. *Becoming Certain through the Perspective*   32
       i. *The Play of Experience*   32
       ii. *Experience is Open-Dimensional*   34
     b. *Accustoming Yourself to the Perspective*   35
     c. *The Way of Life*   40
       i. *The Intrinsic Freedom of the Passions*   40
       ii. *The Way of Living which Masters Appearances*   42
       iii. *Making Your Free Behavior the Path*   44
     d. *The Result: Abandonment of Hope and Fear*   47
   3. How to Integrate Experiences after Meditation   50
C. Reserving the Teaching by Not Broadcasting It   53

Epilogue   53
Postscript   54
Concluding Thoughts   54
Colophon   55

Commentary   57
Self-knowledge   57
Being True to Yourself   62
Different Paths   65
   Renunciation and Transformation   66
   Intrinsic Freedom   69

Appendices   79
A. The History and Structure of the *kun byed rgyal po*   79
B. Quotations from the Root Text   89

Glossary   91

Further Readings   95

Index   99

Preface

During a visit to the United States in 1980, Namkhai Norbu spoke of a very famous text—the *kun byed rgyal po*, the fundamental tantra which introduces dzogchen teachings. He described the importance of this tantra and expressed his wish that it be translated into English.

Due to the size and complexity of such an undertaking, we thought it more expedient and perhaps more appropriate at this juncture in time to translate a related text: Longchenpa's synopsis and practical guide to the tantra (The Jewel Ship: A Guide to the Meaning of Pure and Total Presence, the Creative Energy of the Universe, *byang chub kyi sems kun byed rgyal po'i don khrid rin chen sgru bo*). We have added a general introduction which addresses some of the issues central to the text and, by extension, to life. We hope this will provide a bridge to the text itself. Namkhai Norbu, in addition to inspiring the publication, has graciously written a textual introduction and an historical appendix for this publication. A commentary elaborating some of the key elements of dzogchen teachings follows the text. We have Anglicized some Tibetan words and names, such as dzogchen and Longchenpa. For the second edition, we have updated the Further Readings and corrected minor errors.

We are grateful to Dr. H.V. Guenther, Brian Cutillo, Hiroshi Sonami, Kimberley Peterson, Ken Bradford, Anne Klein, and Carlin

Preface

Diamond for providing helpful advice and constructive criticism during the course of preparing this work for publication and to the Dzogchen Community for helping to fund the first edition.

Kennard Lipman
Merrill Peterson

Textual Introduction

by Namkhai Norbu

The *kun byed rgyal po*

The *kun byed rgyal po* (The Supreme Ordering Principle in the Universe) is the most important text of the section of works of the old tradition dealing with the state of pure and total presence.[1]

The concrete meaning of *kun byed rgyal po* is the state of pure presence that is the actual basis of any given individual. In the well-known terminology of buddhism this is called "the nature of mind."

What is the significance of this absolutely essential text and the meaning of its title? First of all, it clearly shows how individuals who have not felt this state of pure presence can directly experience it. Second, it instructs individuals who have had some experience of this state to become stabilized in the experience and therefore become more certain about it. Third, it shows how individuals with this certainty can, through an even more profound understanding, expand this state of contemplation to encompass their whole life-world. Since this special text is concerned with, and is able to provide for, such experiences, it bears the title, "The Supreme Ordering Principle in the Universe."

For these reasons, it alone, among the three classes of instruc-

---

1. Tib. *sems phyogs.*

tions found in the nyingma mantric literature, is the basis of the dzogchen teaching of the series dealing with the state of pure and total presence. (The three classes of instruction are: the anuyoga, represented by the *'dus pa'i mdo*; the mahāyoga, represented by the *sgyu 'phrul drwa ba gsang ba'i snying po*; and the above-mentioned section of works dealing with the state of pure and total presence, i.e., dzogchen or atiyoga as a whole.)[2] In this regard, for example, we find this text in the Beijing edition of the Tibetan buddhist canon as the sole representative and root text of all the dzogchen tantras and agamas.[3]

Tantra, Sutra, and Agama

The term 'tantra,' as used in buddhism, indicates a text which perfectly presents the profound mystery of the mantrayāna. A text which contains the ten essentials of tantrism—outlook, meditation, behavior, initiation, mandala, charismatic activity, commitments, capacities, worship, and mantras—is known as a 'root tantra.' A text which expands upon and clarifies these essentials is known as an 'explanatory tantra,' while one which focuses on a particular essential is known as a 'branch tantra.' Finally, a text which presents the core of a tantra, or some unclarified part of a root tantra, is known as an 'appended tantra.' These various texts are the basis for the esoteric mantrayāna teaching. Therefore, the colophon of the *kun byed rgyal po* gives its title as, "A tantra about the state of pure and total pres-

---

2. *The nyingmapa* divide tantric literature into *mdo*, *sgyu*, and *sems*. *mdo* refers to the principle tantra of the anuyoga mentioned above and *sgyu* refers to the principle tantra of the mahāyoga. *sems* here is short for *byang chub sems* (Skt. *bodhicitta*), the state of pure and total presence, which is a synonym for *rdzogs chen*, the third group of teachings in this triad. *rdzogs chen* itself is further divided into three series, *sems sde*, *klong sde*, and *man ngag sde*. Our text, the *kun byed rgyal po*, is the fundamental tantra of the *sems sde*. Once again, *sems* here is short for *byang chub sems*, so *sems sde* means 'the series dealing with the state of pure and total presence.' See also *The Crystal and the Way of Light* and *Primordial Experience: An Introduction to rDzogs Chen Meditation*.

3. Beijing ed. Tokyo/Kyoto, 1956, no. 451, v. 9, 93,1.1, 1–126,5,3. Hereafter B.

ence, the supreme ordering principle in the universe, whose point of view, like space, has no center or periphery".[4]

Although tantras of dzogchen such as this one (or the *klong chen rab 'byams rgyal po'i rgyud*, the fundamental text of the *klong sde*;[5] or the *sgra thal 'gyur*, the fundamental text of the *man ngag sde*,[6]) are known as 'root tantras,' some people feel that they are not, since they do not in fact contain the ten essentials of tantrism. This way of thinking is quite narrow-minded. For example, according to the sutric teaching of buddhism, those who accept the four principles of frustration and suffering, impermanence, openness, and nonessentiality, are counted as buddhists. In regard to these the 'four signs which indicate the buddhist point of view'[7] indeed form the foundation of buddhist teaching. However, when individuals who possess greater spiritual acumen practice yogatantra, they take as their primary object the cultivation of the 'two stages' and the actualization of their unity.[8] Individuals with still greater capacity and perseverance who follow the esoteric 'path of appropriate action,' in turn must adhere to the 'four impressive encounters' as indicators of their way.[9] Each path has its respective defining principles and corresponding terminology by which its followers are bound.

In the esoteric mantrayāna, it is necessary to actualize the unitary state of vajradhara by first cultivating the development and completion stages. The ten essentials of tantra mentioned above must be present in this very special path, with its particularly effica-

---

4. B., 126,5,1.

5. This is no. 50 in Kaneko's catalog (hereafter K.). See Eiichi Kaneko, *Kotantora zenshu kai mokuroku* (*A Complete Catalog of the rNying ma rgyud 'bum*) (Tokyo: Kokusho Kangyokai, 1982).

6. K., no. 155.

7. These four are: Everything is transitory; everything transitory is unsatisfactory; there is no essence which makes anything what it is; and nirvana is peace.

8. See our commentary, p. 66ff., as well as Guenther, *Treasures on the Tibetan Middle Way* (Berkeley: Shambhala Publications, 1969), pp. 28ff., 67ff., 94–95, 140ff., and Guenther, *Life and Teachings of Naropa* (London: Oxford University Press, 1963), pp. 138ff.

9. See *Primordial Experience*, pp. 11, 106–107; *Life and Teachings of Naropa*, pp. 202ff.; and Guenther, *The Tantric View of Life* (Berkeley: Shambhala Publications, 1972), pp. 57ff., on these four 'impressive encounters' (mudras).

cious methods. However, individuals with the supreme capacity to follow the still more esoteric path of atiyoga have no need whatsoever to base their practice on the two stages and the ten essentials. To think that such individuals cannot reach the unitary state of vajradhara because they do not rely upon the two tantric stages, merely indicates that one is over-conditioned by the tantric way of thinking, and that one does not really understand the nature of ground, path, and goal as distinguished in the tantric path of transformation and in the ati path of intrinsic freedom. Someone who persists in literalism and fundamentalism, thinking it impossible to understand tantra without these ten essentials, should know that texts of atiyoga such as the *kun byed rgyal po* teach the 'ten-fold nonexistence' of outlook, meditation, commitment, charismatic activity, mandala, initiation, stages of refinement, paths of development, clarification of obstacles, and realization of buddhahood or primordial awareness.[10] These texts are quite aware of the ten essentials of tantra.

The real meaning here is that the different approaches are linked to the three facets of our existence: body, voice, and mind. The paths of renunciation, transformation, and intrinsic freedom each rely primarily on one of these facets. It is important to have a broad perspective and understand that this is why these different paths have different outlooks and methods of practice. The term 'tantra' clearly exists in the *kun byed rgyal po*. The terms 'sutra' and 'agama' are also present; there is a colophon which refers to the "eighty-four supremely esoteric sutra agamas whose supreme meaning is the power of space."[11]

It is well-known that in buddhism there are two teachings: sutra and tantra (also called mantra). Sutra refers to the texts compiled from the teaching of the *nirmāṇakāya* Śākyamuni, who spoke to his audience in concrete physical form. 'Tantra' was transmitted by the teacher Śākyamuni himself, or by a *sambhōgakāya* form to a

---

10. Guenther, *Buddhist Philosophy in Theory and Practice* (Baltimore: Penguin Books, 1972), pp. 157–58.

11. B., v. 9, 126,5,2; *The mTshams brag Manuscript of the rNying ma rgyud 'bum,* v. 1 (Thimpu, Bhutan: National Library, 1982), 261.7. Hereafter T.

pure audience of bodhisattvas at their various spiritual levels. The teaching is a revelation to these disciples of their own pure condition (tantra) through the manifestation of primordial apparitional form; of primordial energy as the uncreated sound of mantra; and of primordial mind as sheer clarity without any bias. All of this manifests the dimension of the full richness and satisfaction of experience (*sambhōgakāya*).

In the case of our text, however, the term 'sutra' in the phrase, "eighty-four sutra agamas," does not mean the same thing as the well-known term. Here, sutra means a summary of what is most essential. The real meaning of 'sutra' here is given by such phrases as, "the depth of the key point," and "the unification of core meanings." [12]

The most essential of all the tantric teachings of the old tradition are known as the three series of inner tantras. In the mahāyoga series, which is the gradual approach to the path of transformation, the very being of the primordial condition of the mind that cannot be interrupted is called 'tantra.' Also, since the practice of the two stages of development and completion are excellent means for manifesting this condition, this path of profoundly efficacious methods is designated 'tantra.' In the anuyoga series, which is the nongradual approach to the path of transformation, the actual primordial state of total completeness is revealed in the manifestation of the field of being known as the ocean replete with qualities. [13] Here, it is this which is called tantra, as well as other names, and those worthy individuals who possess a knowledge of it, whether among gods, nagas, humans, or others, distill and summarize the core meanings of this profound esotericism. Among human beings teachings of this kind are called 'sutra' or 'agama.'

In the ati or primordial yoga, which is the path of directly experienced intrinsic freedom, the uninterrupted continuity of unsurpassed instructions on the essential, profoundly esoteric points,

---

12. *gnad kyi don, dgongs don gyi snying po rnams gcig tu dril ba.*

13. *rnam snang gang chen mtsho'i zhing:* This is the dimension of the buddha Vairocana which is described, from the exoteric, sutric point of view, in the *Avataṃsaka Sutra*, translated from the Chinese by Thomas Cleary as *The Flower Ornament Scripture* (Boston: Shambhala Publications, 1984–1987).

given without scholarly jargon, are known as *upadeśa*. The phrase in the colophon of the *kun byed rgyal po*, "the supreme meaning which is the power of space," refers to such a profound point.

Some scholars believe that certain texts cannot belong to the esoteric mantrayāna. They cite such passages as the following from the fundamental text of the anuyoga, (as well as other similar texts in whose colophons the term 'sutra' appears):

> The tantra which manifests the indestructible core of reality, a primordial awareness of the hidden dimension of the mind of all awakened beings;
> The agama which perfects the practice of yoga;
> The sutra which brings together all knowledge;
> The concrete realization of the universal approach to the teachings;
> The sutra known as 'that which manifests a variety of teachings.'[14]

In effect, they are saying that such texts do not know the difference between sutra and tantra. But these scholars are merely agitating their minds with literalism and intellectualism. According to them, even the commonly used fundamental term of dzogchen, *bodhicitta*, should be avoided there since it is a term of the pāramitāyāna. If this is the case, then any term from a lower approach could not be used in a higher one. Such slavery to the words rather than their intended, stipulated, or contextual meanings is unnecessary. In the ati dzogchen, as in other teachings, one ought to go by the four interpretive guidelines: Rely on the meaning, not on the words; rely on the teaching, not on the personality of the teacher; rely on the real meaning, not on the provisional meaning; and rely on primordial awareness, not on judgmental perceptions.[15]

Supreme reality is completely beyond all the objects of logical and philosophical analysis. Beginning with the three gates of our existence, one is directly introduced to their real condition; then, re-

---

14. B., no. 452, v. 9, 126,5,4.

15. See *Primordial Experience*, pp. xi, 146, n.1.

lying on the practice of relaxing into one's natural, uncontrived state, one turns the wheel of continuous contemplation. This is called the 'perspective of ati.' Practitioners who give birth to this perspective, through the certainty of their own experience, will not be distracted from it by the objects of their senses or by creating any conceptualized objects of affirmation or denial. Cultivating the understanding born in oneself through this perspective is the way in which one continues in and preserves it and the state of contemplation. This valuable method of directly encountering supreme reality, the esoteric heart of space, is particularly taught in the 58th through 84th chapters of the *kun byed rgyal po*, which is why only these quintessential chapters are found in the *Vairocana rgyud 'bum*.

Longchenpa's Guide

The text here translated, "The Jewel Ship: A Guide to the Meaning of the Supreme Ordering Principle in the Universe, the State of Pure and Total Presence," is a particularly superior means for experiencing what is of supreme significance, which is like the very essence of space, the profoundly esoteric, key point. Written by the king of dzogchen practitioners, the omniscient Longchenpa, it is a particularly superior guide which clearly makes its commentary in accord with the understanding of the great knowledge holder and master scholar, Vairocana. This text contains no scholarly jargon. Its real origin may be understood as follows: [16] the victoriously transcendent one, the supreme ordering principle in the Universe, manifested out of the ultimate content of what is, activating an indestructible cognitive responsiveness. This was but a spontaneous transformation of its own primordial cognitiveness and that of the five types of

---

16. The following is a discussion of the transmission of this teaching through the three dimensions: *kun byed rgyal po*, the dimension of being, engages in conversation with his own 'cognitive responsiveness,' *sems dpa' rdo rje* (Skt. *sattvavajra*). This conversation forms the tantra which is communicated through the dimension of the full richness of being and the apparitional dimension down to the present day, the first human master being dGa-rab rdo-rje. The first chapter of the tantra, "The Setting," describes this process of origination. See below, p. 28.

awakened ones. This transformation then proceeded into the dimension of the full splendor of reality and then to the dimension of concrete manifestation, where the supreme teacher dGa'-rab rdo-rje was able to grasp its self-evident communication. Due to its uninterrupted lineage, the fragrance of the activating energy behind this profound teaching has not faded since the time of dGa'-rab rdo-rje. Therefore, this is not a text based merely on linguistically generated ideas. The main subject matter of this teaching is given in four parts:

1. making discriminations from the perspective of the teaching
2. transcending limitations through cultivating this perspective
3. overcoming obstacles through the manner in which one conducts oneself
4. abandonment of hope and fear, the result

Since the profound, and especially superior path of ati is difficult to obtain, like a ship made of precious gems, this work is given this title.

A scholar possessing great familiarity with the Tibetan language and analytical knowledge of buddhist philosophy, would still have difficulty translating this profound work. In undertaking such a translation, one certainly must rely on the following interpretive principles as they apply to the profound ati teaching: do not rely on the words, rely on their meaning; do not rely on judgmental perceptions, rely on primordial awareness. A merely linguistic translation would, needless to say, result in something far from the real meaning.

In this regard, Dr. Kennard Lipman and Merrill Peterson are not just merely scholars with a knowledge of the terminology of buddhist thought and the Tibetan language; they have also studied with many worthy Tibetan masters. Dr. Lipman has studied the cycle of ati dzogchen with me. Moreover, he has not just studied the textual knowledge, but has experience in the three profound series of dzogchen teachings. This text, therefore, has particularly superior translators.

With such an excellent translation, those who have either been fortunate enough to enter the gate of the precious dzogchen teaching or have an inclination towards it, may quickly grasp its profound and supreme significance, whose core is like space itself. Having freed themselves all at once with this profound method, I hope and profoundly believe that they will bring great happiness and real benefit to limitless living beings.

> *Written by the dzogchen practitioner Namkhai Norbu on*
> *the Dakini Day, the 25th of the smin-drug*
> *month of the Wood-Ox year and translated*
> *and annotated by Kennard Lipman.*

Introduction

by Merrill Peterson

The Spiritual Quest

Our experience of life is in large part determined by our conditioned belief system: we believe in certain things, cherish particular hopes, entertain specific fears, and generally point ourselves in some direction based on this focus. The teachings in this text advise us to relax our focus and allow the wider perspective of total openness to flood through us and light our world from within. This openness may be as simple as being alone and quiet, at peace. When we are able to relax like this, the energy we invest in maintaining our usual focus is released, freed into its natural condition.

In the process of letting go of a specific focus, however, we tend to let go of one thing, only to replace it with another—something we believe to be more "true" or perhaps more "spiritual." This is spiritual materialism: when we become caught in the external trappings of a religion, we fail to penetrate to the heart of its spiritual meaning and actually live it.

We usually think of experience in dualistic terms: good or bad, enjoyable or painful, dull or enriching, desirable or awful. Even in a spiritual context experiences are evaluated according to how beneficial, transcendent, calming, insightful, or powerful they may be. This text points to experience that is unqualified yet includes and is at the heart of all possible experiences. Many names can be given to

this experience. In the portion of the text that describes its lineage
(pp. 27–29), a number of different terms are offered to describe the
variations in what one person communicates to another. Yet, as language always partakes of dualism, all these various names can never
be more than partial reflections of experience. Elaborate concepts
devised to describe this experience will only cloud its real meaning;
the experience may only be gained through meditative insight, as
the author explains on pages 35–40.

Although the text concerns itself with the inner reality of all life
and thus favors no particular cultures or peoples, some of its meanings are rooted in traditional buddhist cultural contexts. This is
understandable. The author, Longchenpa, a Tibetan and a great
buddhist scholar, assumed that his anticipated audience would be
familiar with basic buddhist ideas. He therefore refers to other approaches found within traditional buddhism and places them in a
wider context.

The text is clear and direct, and requires relatively little background in Indian or Tibetan cultures or even in buddhism. Yet certain passages can be better understood if the reader is familiar with
their cultural context. In the commentary and in the footnotes we
have tried to supply some of this background information. However,
in negotiating these cultural twists and turns, the reader should always try to keep in mind the deeper intent of the text. It is important
to ask what is really meant and how it applies to the overall fabric, so
that the various threads can be woven into whole cloth.

It is the translator's task to be as clear as possible about the
meaning of the text being translated. In the case of a text such as this,
concerned with the optimal experience of reality, the content is primarily experiential—it deals with that experience which pervades
everything all the time. The reader must allow the experiential import of the text to come through. Padmasambhava, master of the
great light, said:

> When exhaustively contemplated, these teachings merge in
> at-one-ment with the seeker who has sought them, although
> the seeker himself, when sought, cannot be found.[17]

17. Paraphrased from Evans-Wentz, *The Tibetan Book of the Great
Liberation*, p. 224.

An Overview of the Text

This text presents the theory and practice of one of the most direct and wholistic teachings[18] of buddhism. Written in the early fourteenth century, the text is arranged as a guide to the meaning of an earlier tantra,[19] the *kun byed rgyal po*, which was translated from an Indian language[20] in the eighth century by the master Śrī Siṃha and the Tibetan monk Vairocana.

Though it comes to us through the buddhist tradition, the real import of this teaching is not dogmatic. Dzogchen has no cultural bias or limitation, it is not bound up in words and language, and it cannot be fully understood with concepts. Dzogchen practitioners can be found not only outside of the oldest school of Tibetan buddhism (which is usually thought to house this teaching[21]) but even outside of buddhism.

The heart of this text is contained in "The Real Subject Matter" (see pp. 31–50). This section presents an all-encompassing vision of reality and includes techniques for experiencing this vision, sustain-

---

18. Tib. *rdzogs chen*, Skt. *mahāsaṃdhi, atiyoga*. This term may be literally rendered as great perfection, absolute completeness, or absolute perfection. It refers to a lineage of transmission, to a system of yogic practice, and to the experience of reality.

19. Although the text is called a tantra, it belongs to a class of texts that is radically different from the many other buddhist tantras, such as the Kālacakra, Guhyasamāja, and Māyājāla. This text does not utilize any of the complex visualizations, breathings, and yogic mastery of psycho-physical forces that typify most tantras. See the Textual Introduction and the Commentary for a further elaboration of this important distinction.

20. In all likelihood, the text never existed in Sanskrit or any of the other Prakrits of Central India. Tibetans, adhering to ethnocentric ideas about the sacredness of the Sanskrit language, often refused to accept any text that was not composed in Sanskrit. This explains the scholarly controversy that arose in Tibet concerning this text and many like it.

21. The *rnying ma*. The Third Karmapa, Rang'-byung rdo-rje, and Padma dKar-po, both of the Kagyu school; the Fifth Dalai Lama, Ngag-bdang blo-bzang rgya-mtsho, of the Gelug school; and 'Jam-dbyangs mkhyen-brtse'i dbang-po, of the Sakya school were all distinguished practitioners of this teaching.

ing the experience, and making the ongoing experience so vivid and ever present that no fears or doubts can assail it.

On pages 32–35 Longchenpa presents the vision. Here everything is experienced in pure and total presence—the universal creativity. Being distracted from this pure and total presence is to be caught up in what buddhists call *samsara*. Yet, if we investigate the discrete phenomena of experience that we are caught up in, these discrete things lose their credibility and become dreamlike.

Longchenpa advises us to pursue this matter until an inner light arises. He urges us to continue by investigating external reality, suggesting we will only find our experience of it. The actuality of experiencing is ephemeral and unlimited yet always full of energy, and the various experiences are merely the play, the dance of this energy.

This is not to say that everything is a mental state; rather, everything is ecstatic pristine awareness and its various reflections, masks, and disguises. The reader is encouraged to compare this light with the bankruptcy of mere ideas and concepts. Even the idea that everything is just a mental state is itself only an idea.

On pages 35–40 Longchenpa presents a specific, formal technique for experiencing this vision. He first advises the student to relax and be open, to go with the flow and let go of trying to think something or obtain some realization. Then, when thoughts arise, the practitioner focuses on directly experiencing the thought process at work, noticing a thought but not reacting to it, whatever its content. At this point thoughts dissolve on their own and the practitioner is advised to rest in that dimension. After some experience of this way of being, the focus shifts to the materiality of the external world, so it too is integrated into that pure dimension.

Thus the student of this teaching learns, in a formal context, to both be aware of and let go of whatever happens, whatever is experienced. Then, in the informal context of everyday life with its unpredictable mixture of disparate elements, an unobstructed flow can be experienced. On pages 40–46, Longchenpa explains how this is so.

Passions, desires, urges, attractions—these are the main motivating forces of samsara. They continually arise in everyday life with its constant stimulation. Yet, as was explained above, the sensory awareness and the resulting subjective feeling of attraction are both ephemeral, pure experience. Direct, relaxed, free experience is all that really arises. Longchenpa says:

> Look nakedly at whatever appears at the moment it appears. By relaxing in that state, awareness—in which there is no grasping at appearances as something—arises nondualistically, intrinsically freed.

Its attractive quality adds a pleasant, beautiful tone to this pure fact of experience. Reality is beautifully decorated; it is full of desirables, a magical land. When the first flash of experience is recognized, no karmic chain of cause and result can be initiated. The various passions burst forth as brilliant awarenesses, each a facet of the total clear-light energy.

The apparent objects of everyday life can also be experienced at the level of their true inner energy. The forms, your relationship to them, your awareness of them—these are the flavors of reality. Acceptance is unnecessary, rejection impossible. This egalitarian attitude can be put into practice in each moment of life.

At first the spiritual quest inspires both hope and fear: hope for success, for realization, for freedom; fear of samsara, of damnation, of loss of spirituality. However, as Longchenpa explains on pages 47–50, pristine experience frees us from all such concerns. When all experience is naturally complete, unjudged, and open, the ever-fresh awareness that is always newly arriving releases all relative, dualistic preoccupations. In the clear expanse of reality, we spontaneously comprehend every thing, every sensation, without dualistic attitudes.

Worries that this experience may fade can be discarded, because, as the text says, this awareness is always refreshing itself, its excitement and energy are forever newly arriving, like the present moment which can never be anything other than immediately present and completely free. You can neither obtain this awareness, nor lose it.

How to Read the Text

In discussing the various aspects of the text, it is easy to become lost in conceptual meanings and implications. But it is important not to lose sight of the main point: the experience of dzogchen, our natural state, present right now, beyond all extremes and limitations. All dzogchen teachings point toward how to directly experience this.

Longchenpa left many jewels; this text is one of them. He wrote it for one of his students and ever since it has been passed on to those who are poised on their spiritual journey.

After reading all the introductory words, the annotations, and the commentary, immerse yourself in the heart of the living meaning. The spiritual jewels which sparkle throught this text are a conveyance, a vessel for going all the way to the supreme jewel, the great light, pure experience itself.

The Jewel Ship

A Guide to the Meaning of
Pure and Total Presence
The Creative Energy of the Universe

The Jewel Ship

The Anthem

Naturally serene, seamless like space,
Embodying wholeness, the unity of ever-fresh awareness and
    its field,
Unchanging, impartial, not biased toward being or nonbeing,
I salute the supreme universal creativity.

Preface

Here I have elucidated for the sake of future generations the
    meaning of the supreme way of life.
This approach to life, which comes from the spontaneously
    perfect universal creativity,
Is the way to directly experience the pure fact of awareness that
    is at the very heart of all experiences.
This approach is *not* a gradual process of self-development;
    with it, you actually wake up to what is, right now.

Introduction

Out of compassion, the truly and completely Awakened One, with his skillful knowledge, enunciated a myriad of lifestyles and approaches to the teachings. In these cases he taught according to the inclinations and abilities of those to be trained. What he taught to the majority of people had only indirect, provisional significance. He did not speak even once about the direct, real meaning.

> Although the teacher, through the three dimensions of his existence,[22] taught about reality in various ways,
> Those teachings were indirect and provisional.[23]

And,

> To lead beings to a path that was pleasing to them,
> During the first revolution the teacher, through the three dimensions of his existence,
> Taught the existence of separate, graduated paths.
> As a way of leading narrow minded people to the real meaning,
> I[24] have been understood in the limited terms of provisional scriptures.

And,

> . . . although the teacher contrived
> The teaching in this way and taught validly,
> Those scriptures are just provisional, not direct.

---

22. The "three dimensions" are body, speech, and mind which ultimately become the dimension of being, the dimension of the full richness of experience, and the dimension of apparitional being.

23. These quotations (in verse) are from the *kun byed rgyal po* and are referenced in Appendix B.

24. The "I" of the *kun byed rgyal po* is creative intelligence itself speaking, otherwise known to the tradition as Samantabhadra.

Therefore the approaches—ranging from those who are content with listening and preaching to those who practice the supreme method of transformation—are merely a means for approaching the gateway to self-refreshing awareness, the pure fact of being aware. Aside from that they do not, in fact, thoroughly comprehend that awareness because they do not transcend the fundamental pitfalls and obstacles.

Oh listen Great Being[25]!
The three revolutions announced by the three teachers[26]
Of the three times have pitfalls and obstacles.
You may wonder how that could be?
The six approaches[27] which lead to definite attainments
Are pitfalls to the state of total completeness.

---

25. This is the "audience" for whom the text is written.

26. This refers to the three spiritual revolutions announced by Śākyamuni Buddha. The first began in the Deer Park near Sarnath, in India, shortly after the Buddha's experience under the Bodhi tree. It centers on the four noble truths, focuses on the nonexistence of a personal soul, and leads to nirvana. Its scriptures are preserved in the Pali Canon and elsewhere. *The Dhammapada* (many translations of this text exist, among them is the one by Irving Babbitt, New York: New Directions, 1965) is an example of this sort of teaching.

The second revolution, spoken on the Vulture Peak near Rājagṛha, began to stress the six or ten transcendent practices, and especially focused on openness—the relative and insubstantial nature of all the elements and experiences in life. Its main scriptures are the scriptures on transcendent wisdom which emphasized an altruistic way of being. See, for instance, *The Perfection of Wisdom in Eight Thousand Lines* (translated by Edward Conze, Bolinas, CA: Four Seasons Foundation, 1973).

The third revolution, taught at various places, revealed a vision of the interconnectedness of all reality, both animate and inanimate. Our universe is envisioned as a brilliant display of jewel light, all elements permeating all others. The Avataṁsaka and Ratnakūṭa sutras belong to this spiritual revolution. The Avataṁsaka Sutra is being published in 3 volumes as *The Flower Ornament Scripture*, (Boston: Shambhala, 1984–1987). The Ratnakūṭa Sutras have been partially published in *A Treasury of Mahayana Sutras*, (University Park and London: Pennsylvania State University Press, 1983).

27. These are the mahāyāna and the lower tantric careers.

Even though you may familiarize yourself with the point of the lower approaches in this life, you will not see the reality of that which fashions everything, the pure fact of awareness, which those approaches contradict.

> Listen! Those who do not thoroughly understand me—
>   universal creativity—
> Are attracted to the diverse teachings,
> And involve themselves in what the teacher, through the three
>   dimensions, intended.
> They very much contradict what I, universal creativity, intend.

Therefore the scriptures of the real teacher, a direct teaching which was not taught by the buddhas of the three times during the three times, have been spoken by the teacher, universal creativity.

> Listen! I am the teacher, universal creativity.
> These scriptures, which are the heart of the teaching and the
>   root of spiritual pursuits,
> Were not talked about very much by the teachers of the three
>   times.
> This unborn primordial state of the teacher
> Was not spoken of previously by the buddhas of the three
>   times,
> It was not spoken of later, and is not spoken of now.
> The unchanging creativity of the universe
> Communicated it previously, will speak of it in the future,
> And speaks of it now.
> The creativity of the universe teaches you fortunate ones
> This direct teaching, this scripture about the freedom that you
>   do not need to strive for,
> This oral transmission of the elevated teaching
> Which gets at the core of reality, neither exaggerating nor
>   understating.

This universal creativity sums up the unique reality which is the core of all spiritual pursuits and teachings.

Listen! The teacher of the teacher, the creativity of the
    universe,
In the midst of his uncontrived audience,
According to this inner source of all uncontrived, quintessential
    teachings,
Describes how everything appears.
When you have understood the unified frame of reference of
    this core teaching,
All other frames of reference will be reflected within this
    creativity that makes everything else possible.
Thus, if you know me—the intelligence of the universe—
You will know the inconceivable truth.
If you know me—the majestic creativity within everything—
You will know and be at peace with the reality of everything
    else.

It is the source in which the inner truth of all approaches to the
teachings are united.

I, the creativity of the universe, pure and total presence,
Am the real heart of all spiritual pursuits.
The three approaches with their three teachers
Do not exist apart from this one definitive approach.
This is the level of the creative energy of the universe, pure and
    total presence.
It is the source of all spiritual pursuits.

List of Subjects

This quintessential instruction in the primordial approach to the
teaching, concerning the creative energy of the universe—the ongoing absolute perfection which is at the very summit of the eight vehicles[28]—has three main parts: the spiritual advisor who teaches it,
the student who follows the teaching, and the teaching to be learned.

---

28. For a discussion of these vehicles see H.V. Guenther, *Buddhist Philosophy in
Theory and Practice*, (Berkeley, Shambhala: 1971). Simply put, spiritual pursuits can

The Spiritual Advisor

Having himself mastered the true import of the state of total completeness and knowing the philosophical tenets and spiritual teachings of both the non-buddhists and the buddhists, the teacher can generate a direct understanding of the heart of the matter in the student's mind. He knows how to show the sublime path which leads the student to realize that quintessence. The student should rely on a person who is not tainted by the distractions of worldly concerns or mere semantic distinctions. Such a worthy mentor is to be pleased by all sorts of gifts.

> This precious treasury, the authentic master
> Who paints black alum on gold to purify it,[29]
> Entices because of his limitless value.

Contrasted to such a true mentor is one who is confused about the meaning of the spiritual teachings and philosophical tenets of the buddhists and non-buddhists. Craving goods and semantic distinctions, delighting in distractions and entertainments, he breaks his vows and commitments. One who leads people who are faithful yet lack guidance down a dead-end path and who pursues material gain through religion moves outside of the true meaning of the primordial reality. Thus he teaches to others mere words, as if they were somehow spiritual. He even lacks the fortune to understand for himself. It stands to reason that this monkey show should be abandoned.

> Innocents, through deception, are seduced to a path that is just
>   an idea,
> With neither time for setting out nor time for realization—

---

be categorized as those which mainly teach renunciation, those which mainly teach transformation, and those which concentrate on intrinsic freedom. See the Commentary for a further discussion of these pursuits.

29. This refers to an ancient chemical process whereby the last tarnishing impurities are cleansed from gold.

How will they be able to seek reality on its own terms?
When following the teachings of a monkey-like master[30] which
    have no logical basis,
You end up believing in a false path.

The Student

In general, the aspirant must have commitment, an enduring self-confidence, a strong love for all life, steadfast trust, and a great capacity for generosity.

This message, which really opens up one's primordial
    condition,
Is beyond all foundations or bases; it is the core reality of pure
    and total presence.
It should be transmitted by those who have fathomed it,
To those who are very trusting, vigorous, and committed;
Who are sympathetically compassionate and do not change
    their minds;
And who would offer their body, offspring, spouse, and wealth
Trustingly and joyfully, yet without desire.
Such students are characterized by their trust and commitment.

Students who wish to understand this teaching revere the master without pride or self-importance and act without deviating from the oral explanation. Able to serve without holding back either body or life, having forsaken preoccupation with this life, they can accomplish their intention. While alive, students will accomplish their aims according to the mentor's instructions and will be able to persevere in their commitment.

---

30. Monkeys are skilled at imitating the antics of the people they have seen, just as parrots can learn phrases and inflections, but neither monkey nor parrot have any idea what these actions or words mean.

One who abandons fame, who is free from pride,
And who acts for the sake of the inner meaning without
    concern for body or life,
Is marked as one who does not transgress the word of the
    mentor.
Such students are given the teaching of the unborn, the
    innermost truth.
When you have obtained the essential teachings,
How can worldly distractions affect you?
When the teachings have been obtained, such a student is
    called one who has achieved according to the word of
    the guide.
With commitments properly maintained, such students are
    given this oral explanation.
After swearing an oath to proceed following the spiritual
    advisor's word
As long as student and teacher are alive,
The student is given the epitome of the teachings: the creativity
    of the universe.

Thus, being mentally unattached, all wealth should be offered to the teacher. The teacher, to complete the accumulation of merit, accepts without desire what was offered and offers it to the three jewels.

. . . in short, even body and life should be offered,
All the more so food, objects, and animals.
Even if they are not needed,
A worthy person will accept them, offering them to the three
    jewels.

The Teaching

The teaching has three phases: the spiritual heritage, which establishes this teaching as believable and trustworthy; the main subject matter, which arises from that transmission; and the proscription to preserve the teaching by not broadcasting it.

The Spiritual Heritage[31]

Listen Great Being!
The history of the teaching is given
Because initial confidence arises from it.

The historical unfolding of the teaching reveals three ways by which its meaning is transmitted:

* Through natural self-authentication,
* Through the medium being the message and the form being the content,
* Through literary composition.

---

31. The spiritual heritage is the lineage by which the core experiential meaning of a given teaching comes down to us. This refers not only to how it has been transmitted from generation to generation but to how the initial revelation occurred. This is the ontological question: What is the structure of the universe, and how can the beings in it come to understand this structure? The *trikāya* is a description of this structure. The *dharmakāya*, here referred to as the supreme ordering principle of the universe or the dimension of being, communicates and encodes itself into the archetypal forms known as the *sambhōgakāya*, the dimension of the full richness of being, usually symbolized by the buddhas of the five families, with their symbolic colors and correspondences. These symbols communicate themselves to the human level in a way which depth psychologists since C. G. Jung are only beginning to understand. These symbolic forms can be decoded into language by those capable of understanding them, the *nirmānakāya*, such as dGa'-rab rdo-rje.
   A great deal of importance is placed on lineage for maintaining the living spirit of the teaching, and many individualistically-minded Westerners react against this. It is quite right to react when this lineage is the hierarchy of a church or sect, which it is not. Part of this reaction may also be due to an unconscious (or conscious) protestantism that demands no intermediaries between God and the individual. The reality of lineage allows for individuals to receive teachings through visionary or other revelations. The large quantity of hidden treasure teachings (*gter ma*) attest to this. But the individuals who receive such revelations have also been part of a lineage in the more conventional way. It would be nice to have a society, or at least significant groups, of such extraordinary individuals; but for that we must perhaps wait for another Golden Age. See also our thoughts on tradition in the Commentary.

The meaning of this is as follows: (1) out of the total field of experience, the non-localizable realm of genuine reality that is a vast expansiveness free from all fabrications, the supreme ordering principal of the universe, manifests reflecting the deep structure of what is. In this realm which is an immense palace terraced with light he communicates by activating an indestructible cognitive responsiveness out of the ever-fresh awareness which is his own primordial state and that of the five buddhas. This process then proceeds into the dimension of the full richness of being which communicates its message through its own medium (2) to dGa-rab rdo-rje, in the material dimension. He spoke correctly and grammatically (via language) (3) to the great master Mañjuśrīmitra. He nondually communicated the dynamic meaning to the great master Śrī Siṃha. He communicated the very secret heart of the matter to the miraculous translator Vairocana.[32] He communicated the great nondual pristine awareness to the prince g·Yu-gra snying-po. He communicated the effortless field of reality to lCog-ro skyes-bzang legs-smin. He communicated the unchanging ground to rBa rgyal-ba'i dbang-po. He communicated the sky simile to mTshur-mchog-gi bla-ma. He communicated the great settling into the natural condition to Drung ye-shes dbang-po. He communicated the nondual nature to Zur-ston rin-chen grags-pa. He communicated the primordially pure fact of being to lCe dga'-ba'i dbang-po. He communicated the unique fact of awareness that is without affirmation or negation to sNyan rin-chen rtse-mo. He communicated the actual state of things that is totally beyond the intellect to Chos-rje kun-dga' don-grub. He communicated what is uncontrived, unstained, and self-arising to sLob-dpon gzhon-nu don-grub.[33] He communicated the primordial freedom beyond cause and effect to Klong-chen rab-'byams-pa,[34] the practi-

---

32. The root text, which Longchenpa here summarizes, was said to have been translated from the language of Uḍḍiyāna into Tibetan by Śrī Siṃha and Vairocana.

33. Longchenpa's teacher, sLop-dpon gzhon-nu don-grub, is mentioned in *The Blue Annals* (p. 202). Longchenpa's biography (*mthong ba don ldan*, p. 105) says that he heard the *rnying ma'i rgyud 'bum*, the *'dus pa'i mdo*, the *sgyu 'phrul*, the *sems phyogs*, and other texts from the master gZhon-nu don-grub. The *kun byed rgyal po*, which Longchenpa here quotes and structures, is the first text in the *rnying ma'i rgyud 'bum*.

34. The author of this text.

tioner of the natural state of total completeness. He communicated this to 'Jam-dbyangs kun-dga' rgyal-mtshan. He communicated this to mTshugs-med chos-rje rin-po-che rāja.

The Main Subject Matter

The second phase, the actual teaching transmitted by the foregoing lineage, has three parts: the foundation, guruyoga; the real subject matter, setting forth the teaching; and how to integrate experiences after meditation.

Guruyoga

The necessary foundation for recognizing for oneself the reality of pristine awareness, which is what mind is all about, is the phase of yogic meditation on the guru.[35]

Swiftly moving pristine awareness, free of all mentation,
Is like a precious jewel which comes from all spiritual friends.
Not objectifiable, not dependent on transformation,
It naturally satisfies all wishes.
While if analyzed it doesn't exist, when you find yourself in that
    state it really does arise.
Concretely it isn't apparent, yet in its aspect of arising it can be
    shown to all.
The precious treasury, the wise sage who is free of bias toward
    self or other,
Teaches by means of selflessness and compassion, and is called
    'That which accomplishes everything.'

The Visualization and Guruyoga

Now sit down on a comfortable seat. After taking refuge, generating compassion which is not limited to any specific object, and re-

---

35. See the commentary, pp. 62–65.

calling the ultimate content of what you are, which is atemporal and does not come into being, you should visualize a deep blue *Hūṃ* emanating light rays. These symbolize the non-duality of the nature of one's own mind and body. This light, through its vast matrix of rays, purifies all that presents itself internally or externally within the subject-object dichotomy. Thereby all that presents itself is seen as the gods and goddesses in the highest realm.

In that realm visualize yourself as a deep blue Vajra-being with one mouth and two hands, bedecked with silks and jewels, and seated in the heroic posture of such a being. In your right hand is a vajra held against the heart; your left hand is at your side, holding a bell. Imagine a matrix of light rays spreading like rainbows from your heart to the ten directions. On the crown of your head visualize a lotus stalk where a jewel-encrusted lion sits. Seated on this lion is the master who gives you your basic inspiration as the embodiment[36] of the creativity of the universe. His body is blue, he has one mouth, and his two hands form the gesture of meditative equanimity.[37] He is the dimension of totality, ornamented by the symbol of freedom from any fabrications and thus appearing without clothes, seated in the vajra posture,[38] entirely essenceless.

Now imagine the masters of the lineage[39] appearing as a mass of light in the forms of the countless buddhas of the five families, each one fully ornamented in their own fashion, and entirely essenceless. On the tips of light rays spreading from those buddha bodies to the ten directions of the world imagine the dimension of the full rich-

---

36. The master who first wakes you up to your primordial condition by transmitting a teaching such as this one is here visualized in the anthropomorphic form of the supreme creativity of the universe, symbolizing the *dharmakāya*, the fundamental dimension of reality. See the Commentary, p. 62ff.

37. In this gesture, the hands are folded in the lap with the thumbs touching.

38. In this posture, the legs are crossed, with the left leg beneath the right.

39. The masters who have transmitted this teaching from generation to generation are here visualized in the form of the dimension of the full richness of being, the dimension of archetypes. The Jungian archetype, however, is a confusing mixture of experiences of such a spiritual dimension together with many psychological projections on it.

ness of being and the forms of the six sages, who are the magical dimension appearing for the benefit of the world.[40] While vajra breathing recite the mantra *Ōm Āḥ Hūṃ* for as long as you are able.[41] Then everything vanishes into the supreme ordering principle of the universe; while residing in the realm that is essenceless, recite *Āḥ* countless times. After that, having said "May all the phenomena of samsara and nirvana be liberated into the primordial sphere," you may rise. This is a highly esoteric and most excellent exercise.

By training in this visualization for a fortnight, from the realm which realizes random appearances to be like a dream or a mirage, there emerges the self-arising compassion which focuses on sentient beings as well as the realization that all phenomena lack identity.

Thereafter, no mental state will arise which is caught up in the distractions of this life or the eight worldly concerns.[42] Firm disgust for samsara and the determination to get out of it arise as well. These all emerge as the self-manifestation of the primordial state of creativity.

The Real Subject Matter

The real subject matter, the way the teaching is set forth, has four parts: (1) becoming certain through the perspective of the teaching; (2) transcending limitations through accustoming yourself to this perspective; (3) overcoming obstacles through the way you conduct your life; (4) abandoning hope and fear—the result.

---

40. The six sages are the concrete manifestation of buddhahood in the six realms of worldly existence (gods, demi-gods, humans, animals, hungry ghosts, hell-beings); i.e., the dimension of apparitional being.

41. In this practice the *Ōm* is pronounced as the breath is inhaled, the *Āḥ* as it is held momentarily, and the *Hūṃ* upon exhalation.

42. These are traditionally listed as expectations and fear, success and failure, wealth and poverty, praise and blame.

Becoming Certain through the Perspective

Becoming certain has two parts: (1) certainty that what appears is the play of experience itself; (2) determining that experience itself is open.

The Play of Experience

All experiences and life-forms cannot be proven to exist independently of their being a presence before your mind, just like a lucid dream.

> All that is has me—universal creativity, pure and total
> presence—as its root.
> How things appear is my being.
> How things arise is my manifestation.
> Sounds and words heard are my messages expressed in sounds
> and words.
> All the capacities, forms, and pristine awarenesses of the
> buddhas;
> The bodies of sentient beings, their habituations, and so forth;
> All environments and their inhabitants, life forms, and
> experiences;
> Are the primordial state of pure and total presence.

Not realizing that everything is nothing other than the manifestation of one's mind is called *samsara*.

> Without understanding me, the creativity of the universe,
> But investigating the phenomena that I manifest,
> You perceive everything dualistically due to your attachment
> and longing.
> Impermanent, apparitional things will fade away.
> They are aimless, like a blind man.

Accustom yourself to this nondual reality where the duality of mind and that which appears before mind are like a dream.

All that is experienced and
Your own mind are the unique primary reality.
They cannot be conceptualized according to the cause and
    effect systems of thought.
Investigate your mind's real nature
So that your pure and total presence will actually shine forth.

The concrete states of matter—solids, liquids, and so forth—should be examined in this way. Remaining for ten days where no otherness can be found, you will realize that not even an atom's worth of anything exists that is separate from pure and total presence. Realizing that, you will certainly be free from all fabricated obsession with the otherness of objects. Moreover, the very being of what is experienced externally, in being an essenceless, open dimension, is shown to be the state of pure and total presence. In being the variety of unceasing experience, it is shown to be the play of pure and total presence. This is not the same as claiming that whatever you experience is mental because what you experience is not a mental event but arises as the play of the state of pure and total presence.[43] That claim does not distinguish between mind and the state of pure and total presence. The state of pure and total presence is the clear light, the pure fact of awareness, non-conceptual ever-fresh awareness; whereas mind is the motivating factor of samsara: pervasive conceptualization. As The Two Truths[44] says:

Mind and mental events are concepts, mere postulations within the three realms of samsara.

Whenever the state of pure and total presence is recognized, mind and mental events cease. Mind is objectification; pure and total pres-

---

43. A detailed discussion of this topic can be found in Primordial Experience.
44. This text, written in Sanskrit by Jñānagarbha during the 8th century C.E., deals with relative and absolute realities. (Jñānagarbha's Commentary on the Distinction Between the Two Truths, translated by Malcolm David Eckel, Albany, NY: State University of New York Press, 1987.)

ence does not objectify. Therefore, even the subject which is held to be mental is also seen to be the originally pure state of being.

Experience is Open-Dimensional

Because we are unagitated within, there is no object to seek within.
Since there is no attachment to an object, there is no object to seek as a support.
With the compassion which does not arise, does not cease, and is selfless,
Being-for-others is always available. It does not need to be brought about.

Therefore, examine this present mindful awareness internally, externally, and in between. First, where does it come from? Where does it rest now? Finally, where does it go? Can you determine its color or shape? Wherever this awareness is present, is it an object which appears externally? Is it one of the psychological constituents of a person? Does it exist somewhere in between? Since you have not found this awareness by examining and analyzing what appears externally or internally, you ought to conclude that even the ten essential aspects of tantra[45] are also not found upon inquiry. When you investigate whether perspective, meditation, commitment, charismatic activity, mandala, empowerment, stages of cultivation, paths to traverse, obstacles to purify, pristine awarenesses, or buddha activity exist in their own right or are founded on something else and do not find any of these to exist in reality, this is known as "The great transcendent nonmeditation, the real significance of the ten primordially pure aspects of tantra."

[Because my creativity is beyond all affirmation and negation,][46]

---

45. See the Textual Introduction, pp. 3–4.

46. Brackets around verses from the *kun byed rgyal po* indicate portions of the root text which Longchenpa did not quote. They have been included in the translation for added clarity.

I determine all events and meanings.
Because no objects exist which are not me,
You are beyond perspective or meditation.
Because there does not exist any protection other than me,
You are beyond charismatic activity to be sought.
Because there is no state other than me,
You are beyond stages to cultivate.
Because in me there are, from the beginning, no obstacles,
You are beyond all obstacles; self-arising pristine awareness
    just is.
Because I am unborn reality itself,
You are beyond concepts of reality; subtle reality just is.
Because there is nowhere to go apart from me,
One is beyond paths to traverse.
[Because all buddhas, sentient beings, appearances,
Existences, environments, and inhabitants]
Arise from the quintessential state of pure and total presence,
One is beyond duality.
Because self-arising pristine awareness is already established,
One is beyond justifying it; the transmission of this great
    teaching provides a direct entry into understanding.
Because all phenomena do not exist apart from me,
One is beyond duality. I fashion everything.

According to the capacities of the individual, this will be recognized
in three, five, or eleven days.

Accustoming Yourself
to the Perspective

After having become certain by means of this perspective, which
is based on the absence of any partiality in the pure fact of awareness, begin by relaxing your body and mind in a solitary place.
Abandon fear and haste. Seated in the seven-point meditation posture of Vairocana, having been instructed by the master, relax in the
ongoing state of complete self-settledness without hope, fear, contri-
vance, or addition. This is majestic utter sameness—that pure fact of
being where mind and what appears are primordially pure. This

itself is the deep experience of the inconceivable, fundamental dimension of reality.

> Listen, great being, understand in this way:
> The way things appear are one in their pure fact of being.
> Do not make any corrections here.
> This king, uncontrived sameness,
> Is the conceptless deep experience of the fundamental
>   dimension of reality.
> Simply stay with that.

Thus you should let the mind, which is present right now, *be* in this total sameness of primordial purity that is like the sky and is free of any effort of body, speech, or mind. Relax the mind in that naked state of presence which exists when you are not caught up in whatever objects may appear. Then there arises, without any intellectual elaboration, an ongoing lucidity which is not caught up in any appearances or concepts. This is the deep experience of creativity, the primordial freedom of mind itself.

> Listen, vajra being, now practice correctly.
> When meditating on pure, unborn reality
> What appears is neither concretized nor latched onto.
> Because what appears never becomes what it seems to be and is
>   intrinsically free,
> By realizing how things are you are freed without having to
>   meditate on emptiness.

This is the deep experience of "self-originating clear light."

> In this bliss which, in its very being, is free from concepts
> There is nothing to objectify, seek, or contrive with body,
>   speech, or mind.
> There is nothing to focus on or characterize.
> Just relax in the reality of this blissful self-generating pristine
>   awareness.
> This is the deep experience of self-originating clear light.
> This is the activity, in its deepest sense, of the majestic
>   creativity which fashions everything.

Settle into this uncontrived, stainless intrinsic clarity for as long as possible. Whatever thought arises in this dimension should be looked at nakedly. Rest there. By being right there, that thought, without having to be eliminated, is released. Remaining with that state of contemplation, the thoughts release themselves right away like a drawing on water.

> In the uncontrived state of the victorious ones,
> Whatever mental states and thought processes arise never
>   become what they seem to be.
> If you know that this is the situation
> You are free from all notions about striving.

And,

> All the movements of mental activity whatsoever
> Do not distract you from the unborn dimension.
> Know that whatever thoughts arise are meditation,
> Even when not meditating, you will not be distracted.

Then you can gradually enter the realms of the elements—fire, water, earth, wind, and space—introducing those elements into their natural, nonconceptualized condition.

> Listen! Your state of pure and total presence,
> And all sentient beings of the three realms,
> Are clearly shown to be the teacher.
> Because you have not seen your mind as the teacher,
> Even after 100,000 aeons,
> When I, the majestic creativity of the universe,
> Manifest as the teacher, your own mind,
> You should listen to this message: your own mind is the
>   teacher.
> Out of the state of pure and total presence, the impetus for
>   everything
> From which come the five great elements whose very being is
>   this state,
> I, the creativity of the universe,
> Arise as the teacher, in five forms of pure and total presence.

Their dimension is the full richness of being.
Their message is conveyed through their form.
The teacher teaches its own nature.
The teacher, the dimension of the full richness of being,
Cannot be conceived of in terms of identity or difference.
The five forms of the state of pure and total presence
Show everything to be the truth itself.

The pristine awareness which belongs to the state of pure and
    total presence,
Manifesting as the teacher in the form of the elements earth,
    water, fire, and wind,
Does not teach by means of words and letters.
The one who teaches its own nature
Cannot be conceived of in terms of self or other
And teaches the state of sameness and non-conceptuality.
All the beings of the three realms,
Realizing this, become equal to all the buddhas.
Sought-after truth is found by not seeking it.

The pristine awareness which belongs to the state of pure and
    total presence,
Manifesting as the teacher in the form of the element space,
Does not teach by means of words and letters.
The one who teaches its own nature
Cannot be conceptualized as self or other
And teaches the state of nondivisiveness.

These teachers, manifesting themselves among
All beings of the three realms,
Teach by means of their own forms;
By this everyone understands.

Listen, because all you beings of the three realms
Were made by me, the creativity of the universe,
You are my children, equal to me.
Because you and I are not separate,
I manifest in you.

The five teachers who are my very being,
Although they have five facets, are shown to be one.
As that one is me, the supreme ordering principle of the
    universe,
You should believe in the same way.

Listen, all you beings of the three realms without exception,
If I did not exist, you would not exist.
When you do not exist, the five teachers also do not come
    about
And this non-conceptual teaching cannot be taught.

Thus, because what appears is understood to be open, by not grasping after whatever appears, understand directly that whatever is experienced arises intrinsically free, self-originated, uncontrived, and untainted.

In this relaxed state the elements of water, earth (such as mountains), fire (such as the flame of a lamp), wind, and space should be understood in the same way. Through this, whatever appears and all beings will surely manifest in the great naturalness which fosters the state of pure and total presence—the universal creative intelligence.

Therefore, by encountering the elements in this way and by remaining from now on in the dimension of the total natural perfection of all phenomena, faults are primordially purified and all positive traits and opportunities are spontaneously present. Though you still have a physical body, your state is that of buddhahood itself. The scriptural presentation of this says:

In this there is nothing which is not complete.
One perfect, two perfect, all perfect.
Because this activity is excellent, it is pure pleasure.
One perfect means that pure and total presence is complete.
Two perfect means what is made by mind is complete.
All perfect means the excellencies are complete.
Because of this precept of *one perfect*,
You remain in the state of buddhahood.
[*Two perfect* means that whatever appears
Is complete as the magical play of mind.]

All perfect means that
Everything becomes the five excellencies.[47]
Those who live in this state of non-activity,
Though embodied as human or god,
Are this reality of buddhahood.
When acting for the benefit of sentient beings through this way
     of being,
They experience pure pleasure without having to strive.

This passage means that from of old it is predicted that you will arrive at the state of buddhahood.[48]

The Way of Life

This has three divisions: (1) The intrinsic freedom of the passions; (2) Mastering what appears; (3) Making one's free behavior
the path.

The Intrinsic Freedom of the Passions

Even the five sense desires can be understood as the activity of
     pure and total presence.

And,

Even attachment, anger, and stupidity
Arise from the path of that great pure presence.
Even the five objects of sensuous pleasure
Are ornaments of the reality-field.

---

47. The five excellencies are the teacher, the message, the audience, the site,
and the time. All five define spiritual communication. When whatever is experienced appears as these five excellencies, this situation is known as a *mandala*, or
integrated structure organized around a unifying center.

48. Early buddhism contains many stories about people who received a
prediction from a buddha about their attainment of buddhahood. The reading of
this passage serves to predict that the practitioner will arrive at the state of
buddhahood.

And,

> When you enter this pure path,
> Unsuitable things which otherwise would be eliminated—
> Even the five passions and the five heinous crimes—[49]
> Are wonderfully the same.
> Nothing, not even sex, is abandoned.

In line with these quotes, there are two subjects here: (1) The way of living where the five sense objects, that arise with the five passions, become ornaments; (2) The way of living where the passions are intrinsically free, unattached to acceptance or rejection.

The Sense Objects Become Ornaments

Whatever pleasurable things arise—whether forms, sounds, tastes, touches, or smells—in their appearing they are like a dream or an illusion. They appear without any truth to them. The forms, or whatever is experienced, are empty. In reality your own mind is an open dimension. The previous section talked about this.

Look nakedly at whatever appears at the moment it appears. By relaxing in that state, awareness—in which there is no grasping at appearances as something—arises non-dualistically, intrinsically freed. Thus, because what appears enhances reality, the objects of desire are ornaments of the reality-field.

The Passions Are Intrinsically Freed

Though attachment, aversion, dullness, pride, and envy may arise, fully understand their inner energy; recognize them in the very first moment, before karma has been accumulated. In the second moment look nakedly at this state and relax in its presence. Then whichever of the five passions arise becomes a pure presence, freed in its own place, without being eliminated. It emerges as the

---

49. The five passions are lust, anger, stupidity, arrogance, and jealousy. The five heinous crimes are killing a saint, killing one's mother, killing one's father, causing dissention in the spiritual community, and slandering the buddhist media.

pristine awareness that is clear, pleasurable, and not conditioned by thought.

Thus, desire becomes discriminating awareness, the unity of bliss and openness. Aversion becomes the mirror-like awareness, the unity of clarity and openness. Stupidity becomes the reality-field's awareness, the unity of appearance and openness. Pride becomes the awareness of utter sameness, the unity of pure presence and openness. Envy becomes the all-accomplishing awareness, also the unity of pure presence and openness.

So then, you do not eliminate passions, as do those who are content with listening and preaching or being independent; you do not refine away passions, as do bodhisattvas; and you do not transform them, as tantrics do—these judgmentally-conditioned passions are pure and transparent in their own place.[50] This is called the spontaneously perfect, universally creative, self-generating majestic pure presence. In this lies the distinguishing superiority of this approach over all others. By means of this sheer presence, whatever passions arise are freed as the facets of pristine awareness. Thus one definitely gets in touch, right now, with the naturally complete state of being awake to one's capacities.

The Way of Living which Masters Appearances

Know the state of pure and total presence to be a vast expanse without center or border.
It is everywhere the same, without acceptance or rejection.
Blend the nature of mind and its habit patterns into non-duality.
Because entities, whether subjectively conceived or directly experienced,
Are present as ornaments of one's own state of being,
Do not accept or reject them.

And,

---

50. This is the distinction between the path of self-liberation and the lower paths. See the Commentary, pp. 65–72.

Because they are not divided into self and other,
The apparitional, spontaneously present objects are the play of
    pure experience.

And,

Listen: this majestic awareness, freely transforming itself,
Displays the integrated structure centered around the inner
    reality of form.[51]
Everything that exists and appears
Displays itself in the space of unborn reality.
In this inner reality there is nothing to accept or reject.
All that exists is displayed by me, the supreme ordering
    principle.

Listen: this teacher of teachers, the majestic creative
    intelligence,
Displays the integrated structure centered around the inner
    reality of communication.
Everything that exists and is designated
Displays itself as linguistic communication coming from the
    unborn field
And is gathered into this inexplicable inner reality of
    communication,
The supreme ordering principle's symphony.

Listen: this teacher of teachers, majestic creativity,
Displays the integrated structure centered around the inner
    reality of awareness.
Know everything thought or attended to
To be the substance of the unborn ordering principle itself.

The realms of form, communication, and awareness of the
    creative intelligence
Are the three naturally occurring, uncontrived integrated
    structures of reality.

---

51. See above p. 40, note 47.

> One who understands the reality of these integrated structures
>   as complete in a moment without having been set up,
> Has understood the core meaning of the spontaneously complete
>   inner reality.

Thus, because all that is present as form, sound, and thought—ever since they appeared in time—has existed as these three unborn integrated structures, from the start live this great natural nonduality without going into any conceptual analysis. Through realizing beings and their worlds to be these integrated structures, affirmations, negations, antidotes, and hindrances will definitely be freed in their own place.

Making Your Free Behavior the Path

Become accustomed to the fact that all we accept or reject, dualistically affirm or deny (such as enjoyment and disgust, happiness and frustration, beauty and ugliness, fear and security, sickness and health, enemies and friends, love and hatred, or whatever), has one taste, thus judgments are reversed.

> Listen great being: do not create duality from the unique state.
> Happiness and misery are one in pure and total presence.
> Buddhas and beings are one in the nature of mind.
> Appearances and beings, the environment and its inhabitants
>   are one in reality.
> Even the duality of truth and falsehood are the same in reality.
> Do not latch onto happiness; do not eliminate misery.
> Thereby everything is accomplished.
> Attachment to pleasure brings misery.
> Total clarity, being non-conceptual,
> Is self-refreshing pristine awareness.

And,

> Listen: this is how to apply the teaching.
> Because all virtue and non-virtue, acceptance and rejection,
>   beauty and ugliness, big and small,

Are one in pure and total presence,
Realize that there is nothing in reality to accept or reject;
Realize that there is no beauty or ugliness;
Realize that there is no doing or not doing;
Realize that there is no center or periphery;
Realize that pure and total presence is without root, basis, or
  origin.

Listen: this is how to apply the teaching.
Do not go against what you do,
Because doing and not doing are unborn.
By knowing this, whatever you do is the unborn reality.

Listen: because the way of life lived according to creative
  intelligence
Is like space, it cannot be measured or enumerated.
Being nondual, it is beyond the limits of existence and
  nonexistence.
This is pure and total presence's way of behaving.
Even the five desirable things[52] should be understood as pure
  and total presence.

The five objects of desire and aversion are also pure and total
  presence.
Understand the five causes of sensation to be the work of this
  pure and total presence.
Understand that the three realms and their life-forms are the
  activity of the nature of mind.
The way of life which does *not* recognize the unborn
Is not the source of the conquerors, I say.

Also,

Listen! I, pure and total presence, the creative intelligence
  which manifests universes,
Do not teach to those who surround me,

---

52. The objects of the five senses.

A reality that can be affirmed or denied.
I do not teach about splitting the unique into two.
I do not analyze that which is beyond analysis.
I do not correct that which is naturally uncontrived.
Let whatever you do or whatever appears
Just be in its natural state, without premeditation.
That is true freedom.

Also,

The way of living according to me, the creative intelligence,
Fulfills all aims by letting everything be without striving.
Because everything is included within this inner reality,
There is nothing to accept or reject.
With hope and fear eliminated, anxiety is transcended.
Whoever recognizes creativity at work
In the state of sameness where the three times are unborn,
Is completely beyond verbal understanding or not
    understanding.
This is the teaching of no acceptance or rejection.

By practicing this self-liberation which is without duality, the castle of antidotes and rejections crumbles. The watchman who attends to the antidotes is destroyed. Antidotes for problems encountered in meditation do not apply here. You are beyond the narrow passage of hope and fear. The spontaneous accomplishment of the state of creativity is without gradual progress and is not based on the three times. Therefore it is called, "completely exhausting mundane existence at the level of extinction into reality."[53] By living this way, you necessarily progress in the perspective and meditation.

---

53. This is the technical name for the fourth stage of *thod-rgyal*, an advanced method of practice found within the mystic guidance instruction of great perfection teachings. See *The Crystal and the Way of Light*, pp. 101–105.

The Result: Abandonment of Hope and Fear

Seek for the buddha nowhere else than in primordial freedom itself, which is rootless and groundless—the pure fact of being aware right now.

Listen: the dimension of being is pure and total presence.
From pure and total presence comes the dimension of being.
Not even a single atom can be contrived.
Therefore the buddha is not apart from mind.

The dimension of the full richness of being is also pure and
    total presence.
From pure and total presence comes the dimension of the full
    richness of being.
The phenomena which arise from mind
Have no other form apart from the dimension of the full
    richness of being.

The dimension of apparitional being is pure and total presence.
Pure and total presence is the five apparitions.[54]
There is no benefiting of beings apart from pure and total
    presence.
All the buddhas of the three times
Do not exist apart from this pure and total presence.
The buddhas of the past have seen and recognized
Their own minds to be this uncontrived state.
The present buddhas,
Recognizing their own uncontrived minds to be uncontrived,
Even now are bringing about the welfare of beings.

---

54. Six apparitions are usually mentioned, corresponding to the manifestation of buddhahood in the six realms of worldly existence; cf. above note 40. However, sometimes the realms of gods and demi-gods are lumped together. The "benefiting of beings" refers to the way in which these buddhas act to bring about both the provisional and final welfare, i.e., enlightenment, of beings in these realms.

The buddhas who will come in the future
Will not teach that this self-arising pure fact of awareness was
    previously contrived.
This present uncontrived state of contemplation
Comes from staying on the uncontrived path.

Therefore, in the sphere of this uncontrived, unsullied reality, the
three dimensions of being and their pristine awarenesses are spontaneously present in their own right, just now, and cannot be constructed or taken apart.

There is not a single state which is not this vast state of
    presence.
It is the site and home of everything.
So remain in this which cannot be constructed or taken apart.
Here it is not necessary to progress gradually or to purify
    anything.

Well, if I am really a buddha right now, are the six levels of realization present or not? They are totally, absolutely present!

The sign of this unceasing, self-arising pristine awareness
Is the utter clarity of the five sense organs.
This is called *the level of light everywhere*.
The absence of any form of attachment or objectification
Is known as *desireless lotus*.
This state of pure and total presence which does not arise and
    is indestructible
I also call indestructible comprehension.
Self-arising pristine awareness is arrayed throughout
    my immeasurable, true nature.
This is known as *the level of the intense display*.
All the phenomena which exist in the integrative structure
Of pure and total presence, my very self,
Are known as *the level of the great wheel of letters*.
Because form, communication, and awareness neither come
    about, nor are they destroyed,
This is known as *the level of indestructible comprehension*.

Here cause and effect are not different.
The phenomena which arise from mind—good and bad,
      acceptance and rejection—
Are primordially nonexistent.
This I call *the level of non-differentiation.*[55]

Though we can distinguish six aspects in this unity, they are not other than the singular dimension of self-arising pristine awareness. Thus we speak of *the one level of total completeness.*

This present awareness, from the very beginning, is without obstructions and does not stir from reality as-it-is. The individual clarity of the five sense perceptions and the individual clarity of the passions manifesting as the five pristine awarenesses are known as the play of pristine awareness. Because they are complete in themselves without having to be sought for, it is not necessary to hope or fear.

Listen: the pristine awareness of the creativity of the universe
Is nonjudgmental and free from all discursiveness.
Serene and insubstantial, like the sky,
We call it unborn.
Without stirring from the unity of self-refreshing pristine
      awareness,
The details of experience are clearly differentiated without
      being contrived.
Whoever fully comprehends and actually experiences this
Is called a *child of the majestic creativity.*

Moreover, there is no goal other than the realization of natural freedom, effortless, faultless, and without defects, the unique fact of awareness, self-radiant and free from discursiveness.

---

55. *Light everywhere* is the eleventh bodhisattva level, *desireless lotus* is the twelfth, *intense display* is the thirteenth, *the great wheel of letters* is the fourteenth, *indestructible comprehension* is the fifteenth, and *non-differentiation* is the sixteenth. For a detailed discussion of the ten lower stages see H.V. Guenther, *The Jewel Ornament of Liberation*, (Berkeley: Shambhala, 1971). The eleventh through sixteenth levels are discussed in the *gsang ba'i snying po* and its many commentaries, for which see *Matrix of Mystery*.

Listen: because I am spontaneously, effortlessly complete,
I make sure that you, realizing accordingly,
Will thoroughly comprehend all events and meanings as I do.
Breathe a sigh of relief in this primordially effortless state.
I, universal creativity, guarantee this.

And,

Listen: because the nature of mind is spontaneously perfect,
I do not teach perfection or non-perfection.
Do not divide pleasure and anxiety into two.
Be free from hope for nirvana and from fear of samsara.

The perspective of the eight causally oriented approaches involves cause and effect; thus, unconditioned reality is relegated to the background. They claim that the buddha is other than the present awareness. This is like saying that by purifying and transforming the sky there will be another clear sky that is other than this present sky. But in our way of looking at it, by saying that this present mind is the buddha itself, and by attending to its intrinsic clarity, incidental conceptualizations are clarified in the dimension of mind as-it-is, just as we clear up muddy water.[56] Therefore this is the path of natural, spontaneous perfection, the primordial yoga in which the three dimensions of being arise on their own.

How to Integrate Experiences
after Meditation

I am going to speak here from my own experience. This corresponds to the oral instructions of worthwhile masters.

The perspective is unbiased and not subjective; the meditation is the intrinsic clarity which frees whatever arises; the way of life is an

---

56. Muddy water is cleared up by letting it alone, by not stirring it up. The mind becomes clear not by stirring it up with more concepts and arguments, but by letting it be as it is.

unobstructed, dynamic flow; the result is the nonduality of hope and fear. Accustom yourself to what these really mean.

However, if you have no compassion and are confused about what is right and wrong, due to a nihilistic conception of openness, this is an error in perspective. When blocked in perspective by this hang-up that is like a dark abyss, petition the spiritual guide, trust in pure vision, cultivate love and compassion, and train your mind in an awareness of impermanence and the karmic consequences of your deeds. If through obsession with how you characterize things you start taking internal and external entities to be credible, apart from their being mere objects of your point of view, you are stuck in a perspective that hankers after essences and attributes. In that case train your mind in the unobstructed absence of any credibility to all events and meanings and learn that whatever arises is like a dream image which cannot be grasped. When the pure awareness that does not reify appearances arises without any bias or partiality, in the state of clarity cultivate its ongoing flow without being distracted.

If you feel dull or sleepy and your thoughts wander to objects, stay in a cool room with a high seat, exert yourself, and do physical exercises.[57] When you are distracted by thoughts, which is a pitfall of meditation, train the mind in not grasping after experience with thought. Then when many thoughts may come, do not remain in an internally calm state, but continue to create many thoughts. Recognize the thoughts as they arise. Then when no thoughts come, without being distracted from this state of utter sameness without judgment, integrate with the mental objectification that emerges when external objects do appear. By doing this, when nonconceptual clarity arises, cultivate its uninterrupted continuity. If you become identified with the sheer presence that comes as pleasure, clarity, and absence of judgment, destroy that identification by training in the proper perspective and examining your condition. In that calm, spacious state where whatever appears is not identified with, there is no striving, achievement, meditation, meditator, or haziness. In this uninterrupted, nonconceptual continuity where openness and clarity are united, train the mind in the dimension that is devoid

---

57. Massage or yoga, through controling the physical body, control psychophysical energy (*prana*).

of any self-identity. Furthermore, it is initially very important to obtain mental stability toward whatever your meditation object is. Afterwards, everything that arises will have a single taste: this is my experience. The calm absence of thought, followed by thoughts arising; thoughts becoming calm; calmness and thoughts arising nondually: these are the lesser, intermediate, and greater levels of familiarity with contemplation.

After that you will experience the absence of credibility about what presently appears. At that time, there can be visions, spontaneous speech, and positive dreams. Then, what appears will often seem unreal, talk will sound incoherent, and dreams will be lucid, while everything you do in waking life will be seen to be like a dream. After that, what appears will be liberated into a clear expanse, talk will resolve into indeterminacy, and dreams will become the natural light. At that time, the state of pure presence will come about naturally. Having interrupted the dreaming process, the errant propensities—the illusory, habitual allurements—will be destroyed of themselves. Because your awareness becomes united with the field of reality that never becomes anything, this is called *being in the state of pure and total presence* as your primordial basis. Of one taste, like space, this is unobscured, pristine awareness, the creativity of the universe. By cultivating the dimension of your awareness that is without any discursiveness, the dimension of pure being, the final reality, is spontaneously present. Therefore the dimension of the full richness of being and the dimension of apparitional being arise from that dimension naturally, spontaneously complete. This is the greatness of self-refreshing pristine awareness.

Being attached to your ordinary dualistic considerations is a pitfall in your way of living. No matter what appears, by applying yourself without being at all distracted from the perspective and meditation, this unobstructed, powerful way of life will come about with the six senses naturally relaxed. Apply yourself without contradicting this.

Dualistic thoughts of hope and fear are a pitfall of the result. By knowing that this self-arising pristine awareness is buddhahood itself, you will free yourself, when in doubt, from the obstacle of hoping to obtain something in the future.

Reserving the Teaching by Not Broadcasting It

This teaching should be kept away from those who are not really interested in it. It should not be taught to a group of more than five people even though they are spiritually mature because there can be punishment by the dakinis.[58] If not kept hidden, there may be obstacles for both teacher and disciple, exaggerations or disparagements may creep in, and this quintessential teaching will decline.

Although in the true sense of this teaching there is no
    acceptance or rejection,
Nonhumans and other beings can make obstacles.
Both inspirations and accomplishments
May fade prematurely or fear may arise.
Through exaggeration or disparagement, this quintessential
    approach may decline.
Thus, do not give it to people who have a negative disposition.

Therefore, by teaching it to appropriate people and keeping it hidden from inappropriate people, the supreme accomplishment will be realized.

Epilogue

At Khangs-ri Thod-dkar[59] my disciple bLo-bzang entreated me to compose these instructions on the meaning of *The Creativity of the*

---

58. In Tibet the dzogchen teaching was often regarded as a threat to the dominant socio-political-religious structure. It can also be abused by immature individuals. Therefore, it was usually taught in small groups. dGa'-rab rdo-rje has summed up the principle involved here with the words: "If the individual is not a suitable vessel (for example, has no real interest, but is just curious), then one person is too many to teach; if the individuals are suitable, then even one hundred is too few."

59. According to Jam-dbyangs mkhyen-brtse dbang-po, who visited it in 1840, this hermitage was located about 30 km SSW of Lhasa near Tibet's five peaked mountain (*mK'yen brtse's Guide to the Holy Places of Central Tibet*, p. 73).

Universe. By this virtuous activity may all beings become that majestic energy itself.

Postscript

Observing the personalities of dark-minded people who do not understand, or who understand wrongly or poorly, those who do understand have minds wide like the sky and are at peace. Still, it is difficult for them to find opportunities for exercising high compassion.

Nowadays we wander in the ocean of existence, covered by the web of obscurations, naturally stupid. In our shortsightedness, although we analyze the jewel of spirituality, we have no time to find what is really essential. Alas, mind itself is the supreme, precious jewel. Much wealth that was long scattered about is now to be found here. Yet we do not take hold of it, agitated as we are by the winds of discursiveness. With no time for release from samsara, although we may wish for this pure and total presence, wherever we are the lonely mind has no time for experiencing this reality. Striving for it we are deceived by hope for something in the future. In this situation, is any true insight possible? You have for many eons fallen into the turbulent ocean of worldly life without benefit for yourself or others. With no time for liberation, who will protect you from this? Thinking thus, foster firm disgust.

Rely on this very pure fact of awareness, the quintessence to be known directly, the ship of jewels, this profound teaching that is difficult to contradict. Thus you will understand the meaning of human life and obtain happiness at last.

Concluding Thoughts

I am not the sort of person who gives to the beings who live here out of half-baked compassion. Lacking the ability to lead beings to a direct experience of this reality, I remain alone in the forest. I am surrounded by many beautiful lakes, plants, flowers, fruits, and a bamboo fence with vines. With a cool house and a happy life, I have obtained the serenity of a peaceful mind. I am not seen by any humans or demons. I just live here on pure water and the food of austerities. Contemplating the nectar of the spiritual guide's instructions, may I give up this body together with its life.

I have completed the clear light of the death process[60] and am liberated into the primordial level of the clear light in the intermediate state. This is the uncompounded unity of the dimensions of being and their pristine awarenesses. May my own welfare and the enrichment of others be spontaneously accomplished.

Colophon

This "Jeweled Ship, a Guide to the Significance of *Pure and Total Presence; The Creativity of the Universe*" was composed by the yogi of the supreme approach, Klong-chen rab-'byams-pa, at the request of my worthy student. I completed this arrangement according to the "Jewel Lamp"[61] of the great translator Vairocana. May this teaching be preserved by Dorje Legs-pa, Rahula, and Ekajati.[62]

Sealed with Joy

---

60. Tib. *chi-kha'*. Tibetan literature possesses numerous accounts of the experience of death and the intermediate transitional states one's consciousness experiences in its karmically driven quest for a new embodiment. Usually three levels of experience are listed: the *chi-kha'*, the *chos-nyid*, and the *srid-pa*. The *chi kha'* is experienced at the moment of death. An advanced yogi, such as Longchenpa, can experience the clear light of the *chi-kha'* before actual physical death. Immediate recognition of this light brings immediate release from samsara. For a detailed presentation see *The Tibetan Book of the Dead*.

61. We have not been able to identify this text among Vairocana's extant works.

62. The text names these three protectors of the teaching whose energy is devoted to preserving its living spirit.

Commentary

by Kennard Lipman

Self-knowledge

Statements such as, "the kingdom of heaven is within you," or "there is no buddha other than mind," are certainly familiar, but do we really take them seriously? Are there concrete methods for realizing the truth of these statements for ourselves, right now, as we are? As Longchenpa said:

> Here I have elucidated for the sake of future generations the
>   meaning of the supreme way of life.
> This approach to life, which derives from spontaneously
>   perfect universal creativity,
> Is the way to directly experience the pure fact of awareness that
>   is at the very heart of all experience.
> This approach is not a gradual process of self-development;
>   with it you actually wake up to what is, right now.

The goal of dzogchen is "the pure fact of awareness"—an inner awareness and self-knowledge that lead to a state of total completeness, which is intrinsic freedom. Dzogchen creates nothing anew but awakens us to what it calls our natural, i.e. uncontrived, state and allows the complete unfolding of self-knowledge and awareness. The path of dzogchen calls for us to recognize what we are right now, without fantasy or deception.

This text aims to reawaken primordial experience prior to all spiritual traditions, drawing on the teachings found within buddhism. But, just as a raft is no longer needed after crossing to the other shore, any authentic spiritual tradition is self-transcending. This other shore is, after all, nothing other than our actual human existence. By stimulating a spiritual awakening within ourselves, and understanding that we must seek this awareness in our day-to-day existence, we will transcend tradition.

Upon entering the path of dzogchen we are simultaneously involved in and freed from tradition. On this path the richness of the tradition becomes an additional tool for achieving self-knowledge. In this sense tradition can be compared to discipline, for it is only through discipline that we experience freedom, and only by following a tradition will we be freed from it. Once we understand this, we will no longer become attached to the particular aspects of the tradition, for we know we shall transcend it. This brings both tremendous self-confidence as well as confidence in tradition. We can no longer falsify ourself by chasing after externals, trying to fit into some tradition-based scheme or image.

Only by self-knowledge can we understand the unity of all religions. Such a unity (which remains vague at this point) can never be expressed in a doctrine. Many people, wary of traditional religions, think they can construct, deduce, or distill the essence of this unity, possibly through the aid of psychology or philosophy. But a true spiritual teaching is not a creation of someone's mind, not even a master's. It is a revelation, a manifestation, and this gets expressed in an interaction between the teacher and those to be taught. Those to be taught can only understand or receive information in terms of their experience, language, and culture, which are always relative. So the paradox: the unity of religions is found in their plurality.

Once people know that their own inner awareness is the goal, they can begin to implement their self-knowledge. That is, when you know your absolute and relative situations, you can go ahead with the concrete task of becoming certain about your natural state by learning how to work with the difficulties of your relative situation.

This is the understanding of the path in dzogchen, the teaching of the state of total completeness: We are not trying to create anything new; there is no idea of making progress in the sense of better-ing ourselves. Indeed, from the point of view of total completeness, such an outlook is an obstacle; it is the outlook of the gradual path where work is done in stages.

The process of implementing dzogchen follows a very general 'plan' of development.[63] To begin with, an individual who has realized this reality must directly introduce you to your natural state. In dzogchen the introduction to the natural state could be compared to a light being suddenly turned on to reveal our entire being—both its absolute and relative aspects. With the light on we can clearly see our natural state and how it manifests, as well as the temporary obstacles to its total manifestation. We gain a concrete knowledge of our personality, physical demeanor, emotional makeup, and intelligence.

But turning on the light does not automatically eliminate the ob-stacles inherent in our relative condition: our health; childhood de-velopment; unproductive patterns of thought, feeling, and behavior; financial status and position in society; whatever we think we are and do. If not attended to, all these can create obstacles in any phase of the path.

This knowledge differs from the intellectual or philosophical knowledge usually associated with the philosophy of a teaching or school. It is more like the knowledge gained from psychotherapy. In dzogchen this knowledge is a means for becoming more certain about the natural state through learning how to work with the diffi-culties of our relative being. Dzogchen does not demand that we latch on to a concept of bettering or changing ourselves, accumulating any-thing, or building up to something in the future. As Longchenpa makes quite clear, even the aim of self-improvement is an obstacle; this aim typifies the gradual path in which the practitioner ascends through many stages. However, especially at the lower levels, we treat ourselves as objects, thinking, I must do such and such in order to change some part of myself, in order to progress further along the

---

63. As indicated by the "Three Incisive Precepts of Garab Dorje," for which see *The Golden Letters*.

path. But who is telling who to do such and such, to become better, and for what end? To become better means to be better at something. Even goodness is regarded instrumentally, as is the accumulation of merit and wisdom for some other purpose: better interpersonal relations, better meditative concentration, better breathing, better sex, better thoughts, better health, whatever.

Antidotes merely mask the problem; they are a secondary means for dealing with obstacles. Obstacles are not barriers to further progress in dzogchen; rather, they inhibit the manifestation of the natural state. Obstacles do not appear in a convenient sequence, so they can only be dealt with as they arise and affect our lives. To understand this is to begin to taste the freshness of the natural state.

With the non-gradual dzogchen understanding of obstacles, we can make use of any means to deal with obstacles, according to our knowledge and abilities. For example, some people say that meditators have no need of psychotherapy. But psychotherapy is a tool for gaining knowledge of our relative condition, and if you do not know how and why you are using the tool you can be either hurt or enslaved by it. If you have a headache, you may take an aspirin, or if you have an infection, you may take an antibiotic; but if you continue to have headaches or infections, and just keep on taking aspirins or antibiotics, then there is a problem you are not confronting, and you may be in danger of being hurt or conditioned by the tool. So, the ideal practitioner of dzogchen knows their relative condition and makes use of whatever method is suitable to work on the obstacles, so that the natural state can come forth. With this comes certainty and the further possibility of fully integrating it into all circumstances of life—sleep, dream, work and play, joy and sorrow—without tying to change anything, without treating oneself as an object to be improved. You just become more certain about intrinsic freedom, for dzogchen is the path of intrinsic freedom. The path is not some prefabricated system to fit into, it is the unfolding of your own knowledge and awareness in its depth and breadth.

Once you have experienced this vision of reality, you can proceed to become certain about it by learning how to relax into it. But in attempting this you encounter all the obstacles that you have to just let be. We usually think in a dualistic way, treating ourselves as some kind of object. We employ various strategies to try to improve ourselves. This is inevitable, useful, and often necessary; but we should be aware of what we are doing. Eventually we will have to confront this way of seeing things as an obstacle to real, unconditioned freedom.

The path is not intellectual knowledge about buddhism, nor is it knowledge about the mind; it is not about Tibetan or Chinese or any other culture or way of thinking, nor is it knowledge about how to do various religious practices. These kinds of objective knowledge are only aids. The path calls for recognizing what you are right now, without fantasy or deception—an often difficult process. Both in and out of meditation buddhists endlessly analyze and talk about the primary passions: delusion, attachment, and aversion. Such analytical knowledge is quite different from knowing the full depth and breadth of how your very own passions operate, such that these passions become a real issue for you. Here also, there is a difference between just 'feeling' that the issues buddhism talks about should be an issue for oneself, and existentially feeling the whole weight of an issue, being caught up in it, at an impasse, in an intolerable situation, where one's hand is forced. If this is not happening, involvement will just be self-indoctrination in the buddhist issues of selflessness and openness. But the path really only unfolds when these issues become genuinely real for you. Thus practice becomes meaningful, compelling, like water for a thirsty man.

Finally, out of certainty we can begin to actually integrate all aspects of our life into this natural state that we have become certain about. Here too the process seems progressive, but there is no striving after something. Indeed, striving is the obstacle, because what we are fundamentally doing on the path of dzogchen is learning how to relax the dualistic charge, the tension which exists between ourselves and the circumstances of our life. Integration means really overcoming this duality.

Here you learn how to maintain the continuity of your natural state in all aspects of life. This means to integrate this condition with all of life's circumstances, a task unlike the previous two phases.

In all three phases of the dzogchen approach, there is no sense of 'progress' in the sense of 'bettering oneself.' Dzogchen is not a gradual path. It has only one, unique level.

Being True to Yourself

In dzogchen the path begins with transmission, usually referred to as a direct introduction to our primordial condition, through its mind-to-mind, symbolic, and spoken forms. It is similar in function to tantric initiation. This transmission is then maintained and developed through guruyoga: a way to stay open to oneself and thus open to the tradition. We hope the following remarks on guruyoga from a depth psychological point of view will be helpful to Western practitioners, although many other explanations could be made.

People often speak of the 'blessing' (*byin rlabs*) of the masters. The translation, master's 'blessing,' can indicate an unconscious infantalization of the master-disciple relationship. This 'blessing' is the archetypal energy of the tradition conveyed to us in symbolic, powerful forms. This symbolic energy has the power to organize our chaotic energies, those energies which prevent us from relaxing into our natural state. For we now experience our natural state as confusion and pain. This is made starkly clear to us, whether we like it or not, in the second phase of the after death experience where, without the distractions of our sense-based experience and thought, our natural state shines through. If a person is spiritually immature, they experience this stage as blinding lights, horrific sounds, and terrible visions. This is because the energies of the psyche have not been balanced and made coherent. Such coherence can occur through the power of the symbolic energies which the tradition transmits in the form of initiation and direct transmission. Carl Jung called these symbolic energies archetypes and named the symbol of a coherent psyche a *mandala* (a balanced configuration of psychic energies).

The most powerful form of archetypal energy is worked with in the guruyoga. In it, one is dealing with the archetype of the Self, one's own wholeness, through the mechanisms of transference and projection.[64] In this case one is not only dealing with the projection of unconscious personal qualities, but with archetypal, transpersonal, elements. Not only does the guru provoke images of demonic/

---

64. Jung's *The Relations Between the Ego and the Unconscious* begins with a beautiful description of the personal and transpersonal aspects of transference phenomena.

benevolent daddy/mommy, but these images are pervaded by the archetype of the Self: wholeness, mastery, autonomy. As Jung always pointed out, although these archetypes are expressed as symbolic images they are the life-energy at work.

The symbolism of guruyoga gives us an opportunity to work with these powerful energies. These energies range from the symbiotic contentment or destructive rage of the infant, to the abysmal fears or sense of self-mastery of the autonomous individual. Working with these energies means using an archetypal symbol, the guru-as-Self, the embodiment of generations of spiritual progenitors, the symbol of our rich clan-inheritance, and feeling its power in our psychic blood and bones. This image is broad and powerful enough to encompass our energies, but it is subtly complemented by the presence of a master, a concrete individual who cannot be seduced by one's projections, even though we (and many others) may project images of god-goddess-father-mother-lover on to her or him. Thus our text speaks of the characteristics of a genuine teacher, as well as student, and there must be an initial testing period in the relationship in which a *mutual* checking out should occur.

Through repeated practice of the guruyoga, a repeated engagement with the archetypal energies described above, all these powerful energies can be organized into a coherent laser beam of light and beamed back on to their source: ourselves in our natural state which is no different from that of the teacher. Then, our state will no longer be experienced as confusion, fear and pain.

People are often confused about the meaning of the term 'guru.' Here, in the guruyoga, one's own teacher is visualized in the form of the entire dimension of being. Is this outrageous glorification? It is very important to understand that the guru means the unification of all transmissions and should not be confused with the personality of the teacher. It is always said, "Rely on the message of the teacher, not on the personality." When guruyoga and devotion become a personality cult, the participants involved have become controlled by powerful archetypal forces, rather than having mastered those forces.[65]

---

65. A Jungian or other analyst, with an understanding that in the guru one is dealing with the 'archetype of the Self,' might be of help here in restoring balance to over-inflated and deflated egos.

So, in the guruyoga and the 'blessing' of the guru, we are involved in the most powerful archetypal energy of all, the 'archetype
of the Self,' our own wholeness. The natural state has an energy; it is
alive. We either master it or, if we are unconscious of it, it masters
us. The teacher both employs and symbolizes this energy. We in-
evitably project this energy on to the person of the teacher. In sutric
teaching one does not work much with the teacher in terms of this
energy, although it is of course present. In tantra and dzogchen it is
the basis of the path. The skillful teacher helps the student redirect
this powerful archetypal projection from the person of the teacher
back to the student him or herself. There are different styles of doing
this depending on the inclinations of the teacher and student. Some
teachers, aware of the power of these projections and the limitations
of the student, allow the projections to develop somewhat and then
wean their students from them. Others cut off the projections from
the very start and turn over to the student the power of the projections for his or her own use. Some students just cannot handle such
abrupt treatment of their precious projections or the energy which is
freed up when these projections are abruptly withdrawn from the
precious object. Projections are intimately bound up with a deflated
or depressed ego: the teacher is viewed as being the all-powerful
spiritual father-mother next to which one is an ignorant nothing. Yet,
at the same time, such self-abasement is the flip-side of a psychic
over-inflation: being one of the 'elect,' being chosen or even favored
by the daddy-mommy guru.[66]

Buddhists talk endlessly about the non-existence of any abiding
principle in our personality. This means that the concept "person" is
inadequate for understanding our individuality. This non-existence
has far-reaching implications for every aspect of our existence. But,
especially in the case of the guru, how can one go on blindly project-
ing this delusion on to the teacher, and then even worship this
projection?

The key point is to be able to experience the archetypal energy

---

66. The two cases of ego deflation and inflation are clearly demonstrated in
the mistaken, sentimental devotion of those who are enslaved by false gurus, or in
the seeming autonomy of those inflated individuals who go out and do missionary
work for the cause.

of the guruyoga as increasing self-mastery. Through the archetypal image of the guru we feel the energies of transference directed towards our own natural state. This process is constantly reinforced by the presence of the teacher in the flesh as a unique, autonomous individual, unwilling to be captured by projections. In being 'just him/herself' he/she is showing us, indeed forcing us to be 'just ourselves.'

Different Paths

Longchenpa's introduction to the text speaks strongly and clearly about the relationship between self-liberation and paths other than dzogchen:

> Even though in this life you may familiarize yourself with the point of the lower approaches, you will not see the reality of that which fashions everything, the pure fact of awareness, which those approaches contradict.

> Those who do not thoroughly understand my reality,
>   universal creativity,
> Are attracted to the diverse teachings,
> And get involved in what the teacher, through the three
>   dimensions, intended.
> They very much contradict what I, creative intelligence,
>   intend.

> Therefore, the scriptures of the genuine teacher, a direct teaching which was not taught by the buddhas of the three times during the three times, have been spoken by the teacher, universal creativity.

Several points should be clarified here to avoid any misunderstanding. First, one path is superior to another because of its method, not its goal. A method is superior if it deals more directly with the heart of the matter: enlightenment, direct experience of the goal, awakening. By using a superior method, psycho-spiritual maturation can occur more rapidly. Second, a method is also superior if it is easier to practice, in the sense of affording more possibilities for practice and therefore more opportunity for maturation.

Different paths are often categorized into the sutric, a path of renunciation where obstacles are eliminated with antidotes, the tantric, a path of transformation, and the dzogchen, a path of self-liberation. The balance of this commentary presents an overview of these paths.[67]

Renunciation and Transformation

The path of renunciation is based primarily on a conventional understanding of the relationship between basis, path, and goal, where the cause precedes and produces the effect, the means achieve the ends. It relies on the intellect, reasoning, debate, proof, and so forth, to establish the meaning of ultimate truth, which is itself the ground, or basis, for the path. Renunciation consists of the practice of calmness and insight. It is gradual; it is said to take eons to reach the goal. We should also note that by explaining conventional truth in terms of our impure sense-based experience of ourselves and our world, we adopt an attitude of acceptance and rejection. We proceed by furthering positive, healthy thought and action, while countering the negative with antidotes.

The path of transformation is not based on our commonly experienced world. Its source is unconventional, a deeper and more subtle dimension of reality, which we can (only inadequately) evoke with the word 'energy.' This energy operates outside of ordinary, linear time with its separation of cause and effect. Thus, transformation relies not on intellectual understanding, but on deep experience of the life-process itself. To do this it uses techniques involving mandala, channels, energy foci, and so on. Its basis is primordial, ever-fresh awareness, uncontrived by the mind. Remaining with this awareness is the path, and making it fully evident is the goal. To make the goal into the path, this primordial awareness is introduced at the beginning of the path through initiatory experience.

Transformation can be pursued in many ways, as opposed to re-

---

67. Readers who would like a more detailed presentation of these paths may refer to Herbert Guenther's *Buddhist Philosophy in Theory and Practice.*

nunciation, which is tied to acceptance and rejection. Tantra uses special methods to transform passions such as attachment and aversion and the bodily energies that support them. Through tantra, passions are invigorated rather than renounced. Because there is no need to accept or reject, all experiences can be used as friendly helpers on the path. But this requires the precise application of the special methods of transformation. If we possess sharp faculties we can understand the esoteric basis of tantra and follow its path, which can lead to realization in our life-time, rather than the eons required by the path of renunciation.

To make the distinction between renunciation and transformation more concrete, let us see how they differ in the three dimensions of our existence: body, voice, and mind.

In buddhism the body is the whole dimension of sense-based experience, both the physical body as well as its environment. Renunciation works with the ordinary body and environment, which is an exoteric approach. Buddha Śākyamuni was an Indian who taught based on experiences common to all of us. He spoke about frustration and suffering; he then explained their source and motivating forces, their cessation, and how to bring about their cessation. In his teaching the body is flesh, blood, and bone, subject to disease and decay, ending in death. It is the focal point of our drives and obsessions and the means by which we enact them. The most one can do on the sutric path is use this ordinary body to engage in ethically positive actions, avoid negative actions, and maintain it as a healthy support for meditation. Ultimately, the body is an open dimension without any unvarying or exhaustibly specifiable mode of being, like an apparition, there yet nothing. This is the most effective antidote to our deluded experience of the body as a thing, as the 'real' cause we believe of our drives and obsessions (such as when we give physiological reasons for our actions).

In transformation, on the other hand, the dimension of embodiment is not our commonly shared world. The teacher is not human in a human world, but the teacher and environment are revealed as a sheer energy manifestation through light, color, and sound, archetypal symbols in the form of a mandala. Through visualizing and embodying this dimension, experiencing oneself as a luminous presence in a palace of light, one transforms one's ordinary situation of the body as the focus of drives and obsessions in an environment of objects of interest. In this archetypal vision the practitioner also performs physical symbolic acts, such as expressive gestures and dance. In this transformation process ordinary experience of the body and environment are cut off. But the body's function as the focus of drives and obsessions is not merely cut off, and in a much more efficacious way than with renunciation, but is transformed.

In renunciation, voice is primarily understood exoterically. Thus, the ordinary voice can only be used to engage in ethically positive speech, such as avoiding abusive language and empty talk, or speaking kind words. To understand speech to be open, not some thing, like an echo, is the supreme antidote to our deluded experience of speech as the expression of our drives and obsessions.

In transformation voice is not only speech or the sounds produced by our vocal chords, but also all the respiratory energy which supports it, which is itself linked to all our bodily energies. Voice, called mantra, is the archetypical, natural expressive energy of the mandala. All speech becomes mantra. Through visualization and controlled breathing, we experience our physiological energies as the energies of a divine presence.

In buddhism mind is the dominant, controlling factor in the hierarchy of body, voice, and mind. It characteristically expresses itself in conceptual thought and judgment, which involves a subtle process of organizing experience into categories and types. In renunciation, calm and insight meditations banish the mental agitation caused by the conceptual activity. Through meditation we ultimately understand that all concepts are without meaning in themselves or in reference to any object; therefore we no longer get caught up in conceptually-delineated situations.

Transformation understands mind esoterically, as the dimension of the nonconceptual meaningfulness of being. Here thoughts are the play of this dimension's energy. Thus, thought is no longer information about a dualistically experienced environment but is ever-fresh awareness, the unconditioned knowing that opens up the whole domain of experience. This is the mandala of mind.

A person may be interested in a path for which they are not suited, or merely practicing the outward cultural forms of a teaching. No one can choose a path for you, not even a master. Personal knowledge of how a method works makes that method suitable for you.

The Tibetan texts specifically state that each path *primarily* teaches its principal method. Buddhism is about awareness and our capacity to know and live that awareness. This cannot be limited by a method. In practicing *vipaśyana* or *zazen* one may perfectly well have understood what dzogchen calls self-liberation. To be more precise, what we are calling a 'method,' such as renunciation, transformation, or self-liberation, does not mean the form a practice takes but *what is actually going on* in the practitioner, *what is working* to unfold the individual's innate, natural state. This depends entirely on capacity. The experience is what matters, not the name or outward form.

Intrinsic Freedom

The path of self-liberation can be differentiated from the path of renunciation and transformation by looking at how the key term *bodhicitta* is defined in each of these paths.

For the path of renunciation *bodhicitta* is defined in relative and ultimate terms; it is both the aspiration to enlightenment as well as the practice of working toward it. Relative *bodhicitta* means to place yourself unselfishly, compassionately, at the disposal of others in a heart-felt desire to remove the real causes of unhappiness. Ultimate *bodhicitta* is the direct understanding of openness—understanding that nothing possesses an unvarying or exhaustively specifiable mode of being. Such understanding definitively ends unhappiness and leads to enlightenment. Hence, the path of renunciation is also called the approach of causality.

The path of transformation defines the term *bodhicitta* variously, depending upon whether it is used in the development stage or completion stage. In development, we transform the ordinary life-world into a mandala, a pristine dimension of light, color, and sound, by imagining ourself as a divine presence in a palace, evoking this reality with mantra, and inwardly experiencing this pristine state through the strength of concentration.[68]

---

68. Technically, this experience is known as the pride of transfiguration (*lha'i nga rgyal*), which is not a form of psychic inflation based on feelings of deification, but rather the countering of our habitual experience of the mundaneness of our

In the visualization techniques used here, *bodhicitta*, understood as the goal directing the process, is present *symbolically* as (1) the feeling of openness, of opening up and out, with which one starts; (2) the pure moon-disk; and (3) the seed-syllable appearing on it out of which the mandala arises. Thus, tantrism is known as the approach in which the goal directs the process. But it is still a gradual path, from the point of view of dzogchen, since one proceeds to the goal by stages using the process of transformation. In the nyingma tradition, this three-fold process of developing the mandala is known as the three contemplations: contemplation of reality as it is, the absolute *bodhicitta*, or *śūnyatā*, the primordial openness of being (*de bzhin nyid kyi ting nge 'dzin*); contemplation of light everywhere, the relative *bodhicitta*, or compassion, radiating out of this openness (*kun tu snang ba'i ting nge 'dzin*); and causal contemplation, where the transfigured form, the deity actually embodying these two forms of *bodhicitta*, is generated from its seed-syllable (*rgyu'i ting nge 'dzin*).[69]

In the completion stage *bodhicitta* relates to embodied felt experience. In this pristine dimension we experience ourself as deity through the *felt sense* of our body's channels and energy centers, which are visualized and felt to be a transparent medium of energy and light. Feeling, even more than visualization (which is related to sight, the most distancing and dualistic of our senses), enables us to transform our passions by controlling their energetic bases in the body. Here, for example, the moon disk is given its inner meaning; it is the male principle within the individual's energy-body. The male

---

world. Mundaneness means the meshing of our drives and obsessions with our environment. This mundane world is taken for granted as the stage for playing out our passions and is continually being used up. Yet we feel there is always more despite the presence of sickness, old age, and death. This is the world of appetite, whether gross, refined, or ethereal. In tantra this world is transformed into a mandala of the *sambhōgākaya*, the dimension of the total richness and satisfaction of lived-through experience, which is not based on appetite but on the five modes of primordial awareness.

69. According to the terminology of the gSar-ma schools of tantrism, these three are called meditation on emptiness which is the accumulation of wisdom (*ye shes tshogs stong nyid bsgom*); meditation on the four immeasurables (*tshad med bzhi bsgom*); and meditation on the mandala (*dkyil 'khor bsgom*).

principle refers to the structuralizing power in the body and experience, symbolized by the moon or *vajra*. The female principle is the functioning energy, symbolized by the solar fire or lotus. Thus, for example, in the practice of inner heat the red female solar fire at the navel is made to rise up and melt the white male lunar moon-semen-drop at the forehead, thus uniting these two energies.

During the completion stage the term *bodhicitta* also refers to the result of the union of male and female energies, which is enlightenment, the goal of transformation. We may sum up this discussion of tantric *bodhicitta* with a succinct quote from David Snellgrove's introduction to the *Hevajra Tantra*:

> Although the two conceptions are essentially the same, one may regard the *bodhicitta* under two aspects: (1) as the consummation of vajra and lotus, when it is envisaged in the mystic state as the moon which melts in the one-thousand-petalled lotus at the summit of the head, and flows through the whole body pervading it with bliss, or (2) as the seed, the source of existence (*samsaric*), and therefore the starting point (*bindu*) of the mandala.

Dzogchen differs from both the sutric path of renunciation and the tantric path of transformation in its understanding of *bodhicitta*. In dzogchen, *bodhicitta* refers to the natural state of the individual; it is synonymous with the state of total completeness and sheer presence. Its special method for realization of the natural state is known as intrinsic freedom.

As in sutra, *bodhicitta* in dzogchen encompasses compassion, in both its relative and absolute aspects. As Longchenpa, quoting from the *kun byed rgyal po*, indicates:

> Compassion does not arise, does not cease, and is self-less,
> Therefore being-for-others is always present. It need not come
>   about.

But from the dzogchen perspective, sutric compassion is contrived, constructed by the individual as the means to an end. The intrinsic freedom of dzogchen reveals that nothing in the individual be constructed or changed. The direct realization of our own inalienable, natural state, our own *bodhicitta*, spontaneously entails compassion, since such an awareness is also an awareness that others are ignorant of the natural state. It must be remembered that, as taught in buddhism, compassion is not just love, kindness, and caring for the welfare of others, but is also a knowledge of the fundamental causes of unhappiness and of the definitive means for uprooting them. Thus, without a knowledge of your natural state, compassion will always be contrived. In the sutra teaching there is no defect in this, since no other method of compassion is available.

Regarding the passions, Longchenpa states:

> So then, not eliminating passions, as do those who are content with preaching and listening or being independent, or refining away passions, as do bodhisattvas, nor transforming them, as the tantrics do; these judgmentally-conditioned passions are pure and transparent in their own place. This is called the spontaneously perfect, universally creative, self-generating, majestic state of pure presence. In here lies the distinguishing superiority of this approach over all others. By means of this sheer presence, whatever passions arise are freed as facets of pristine awareness. Thus one definitely gets in touch with, right now, the naturally perfect state of buddhahood.

What does it mean that, "Judgmentally conditioned passions are pure and transparent in their own place?" Tantrism frees the passions from their judgmentally governed state of conflict by transforming them into their primordially pure state of awareness-energy, *bodhicitta* being the name for the basis and goal of this process. The passions, in their profane form, are understood to be distortions, deflections of their essentially divine quality. They only need to be transformed by an inner alchemical process, which is based on this correspondence between the profane and the sacred.

Dzogchen's method for liberating the passions rests on their intrinsic freedom. Passions are self-liberated, naturally freed in their own dimension, the dimension of the total field of events and meanings. Self-liberation occurs when we realize our natural state, *bodhicitta*, which is the state of sheer presence, the state of total completeness, the supreme ordering principle of the universe.

This understanding of *bodhicitta* (*byang chub sems*) in dzogchen, which in the text is anthropomorphized as *kun byed rgyal po*, literally translated as 'the king who creates everything,' might invite comparisons with Theism. The syllables of these terms are explained in the root text as follows:

The term 'all' (*kun*) refers to all that is.
If it is asked, "What is all that is?"
The answer is: teachers, teachings,
Audiences, situations, and times are all and everything.

The term 'to make' (*byed*) refers to the doer.
Because self-refreshing pristine awareness makes everything:
Teachers, teachings, audiences, situations, and times,
It is the doer.

The term 'king' (*rgyal po*) refers to the very core of reality,
Self-refreshing pristine awareness,
That which makes everything and is sovereign over all.
It rules over everything in making all that is.

The meaning of the term 'pure' (*byang*) is as follows:
The very core of reality, pure and total presence,
Is self-refreshing and primordially pure.
Thus it is the supreme ordering principle in the universe,
    which fashions everything.
Since it is pure in being wholly positive,
It is explained with the term 'pure.'

The meaning of the term 'total' (*chub*) is as follows:
The very core of reality, self-refreshing pristine awareness,
Encompasses everything, pervades everything:
All that appears and the beings for whom it appears,
All environments and their inhabitants,
The three times, all those who have awakened to their full
    capacity,
The three realms and their six life-forms,
Sentient beings, actuality, everything.
This explains the term 'total.'

The meaning of the term 'mind' (*sems*) is as follows:
The very core of reality, self-refreshing pristine awareness,
Knows all that appears, the beings for whom it appears,
All environments, and their inhabitants;
It has power over them and clearly defines them.
This explains the term 'mind.'

Kun byed rgyal po is a name for the natural state of every individual, each of whom is the locus for the nondual manifestation of the field of experience, known as a *mandala*. A mandala possesses the five aspects of teacher (creative center), teaching (message transmitted), audience (receivers), situation (spatial setting), and time (temporal setting). H.V. Guenther has pointed out that the aspect of teacher as the creative center, performs many of the same functions as that of the "God idea" in the West. [70] One occasionally finds clear statements of such a 'non-dual presence' in Western theological terms, as in the following Kabbalistic account as to how the *sefirot*, God's instruments or 'vessels' of creation, manifest themselves out of the 'limitless' (*Eyn Sof*):

> Just as forms are reflected in a mirror, the *sefirot* are the template and form for everything that exists. But they are not additions to [the *Eyn Sof*], just as what is seen in a mirror does not add to it.[70a]

The creative intelligence of the universe-as-mandala is what we would today call the intrinsic intelligence of self-organizing, self-regulating systems, which have no need of an external agent, will, design, or law. Where we experience ourself as an object over against other objects, we call this 'mind,' which is the creative energy of the universe, but not creativity itself, just as reflections are not the reflective surface of a mirror itself. The mirror surface cannot be tainted or transformed by any reflections appearing on it. In this

---

70. Guenther, H.V., *From Reductionism to Creativity: rDzogs-Chen and the Sciences of Mind* (Boston: Shambhala, 1989), p. 195

70a. Isaiah Horowitz, *The Generations of Adam*, Krassen, M., tr. (New York: Paulist Press, 1996), p. 122.

analogy lies the key to understanding the meaning of *bodhicitta*, our natural state.

Longchenpa explains the meaning of *bodhicitta* (*byang chub sems*) as follows:

> The term *byang* is used because Saṃsāra has never been experienced as something existent in view of the fact that the facticity of pure awareness has never been tainted. The term *chub* is used because in this vitalizing power capabilities are spontaneously present, and this is because (its actuality) exists as the possibility of rising as anything. The term *sems* is used because of the fact that responsiveness (to the solicitation of actuality) is present in an all-encompassing way so that by its lucency both Saṃsāra and Nirvāṇa are encompassed, and because it comes as an individual experience. Since the ordinary mind and its mental events with their host of dividing thoughts make their appearance out of the creativity of playful energy in impure forms, they are not *byang-chub-sems*, and since they contradict the latter because they are samsaric mind, there is a great difference between creativity as such and what appears as playfulness deriving from creativity.[71]

Let us comment on this passage word for word. *Bodhicitta* is the natural state, the basis or ground (*gzhi*) of an individual's being. Here pure awareness or pure presence (*rig pa*) is a synonym for *bodhicitta*. Because of its specific understanding of *bodhicitta*, dzogchen has a special method, self-liberation or intrinsic freedom (*rang grol*), for accomplishing it directly, without resorting to methods of renunciation, refinement, purification, or transformation. The natural state is divided into three aspects, which the three components of the Tibetan word *byang chub sems* explain. The first aspect is referred to by the phrase "the fact of pure awareness," which means the pure beingness of the natural state, its essence (*ngo bo*). It is explained by the word *byang*, 'pure,' because, like the reflective capacity of a mirror, it has never been nor can it ever be tainted by the reflections

---

71. From *lung gi gter mdzod* p. 173, autocommentary on the *chos dbyings mdzod* translated by H. V. Guenther, *Kindly Bent to Ease Us*, Part 1, p. 258.

which appear on it. This is also referred to by the terms primordial purity (*ka dag*), and void, empty, open, no-thing (*stong pa*). Thus, from this standpoint, "samsara has never been experienced as something that exists," just like a reflection in a mirror is not something real in itself.

The second term, *chub*, means to realize or understand. It explains how the primordial basis presents itself in actuality, its nature (*rang bzhin*). That is, although the basis (natural state) is no-thing, like the capacity of a mirror to reflect, it is not a mere nothing. Reflections are always present and anything can be reflected. Longchenpa says that "capabilities are spontaneously present." Capabilities (*yon tan*) refers to how our nature manifests itself out of our primordial basis. These are usually referred to as buddha qualities. The term buddha was translated into Tibetan as *sangs rgyas*—one who has woken up to his or her capacities, whose capacities can manifest, radiate, and expand because he or she is no longer ignorant of the natural state. As we have explained, other paths, based on the principle of cause and effect, gradually remove this ignorance to reveal these capacities. But here in dzogchen it is said that the capabilities are spontaneously present. The mirror is not just a pure, open possibility to reflect; it also clearly, effortlessly, naturally reflects whatever is present. Thus, this second facet is characterized by the terms radiant (*gsal ba*), and spontaneously present (*lhun grub*).

One might ask, "Isn't there a difference between the spontaneous presence of buddha capacities and the presence of the impure samsaric phenomena that I experience right now?" It depends on our perspective. The third aspect helps us understand why.

The third aspect, the responsiveness of our primordial state to whatever presents itself, is indicated by the term energy (*thugs rje*), which corresponds to mind (*sems*). That is, we are the locus of being, which is a pure, open possibility, presenting itself in radiant clarity. The process of experiencing, of being open and responsive to what presents itself has energy, momentum. We can experience this energy openly without judgment, or we can become confused and distracted by it and regard it judgmentally. In either case, the energy remains that of the natural state, the primordial basis of our being. The mirror analogy can illuminate this: If we know that we are the mirror itself, we do not experience the reflections judgmentally; however, if we feel that we are looking at the mirror's reflections from a standpoint outside it, then we make dualistic judgments about what we see. This is what is meant by the ordinary mind appearing "out of the creativity of playful energy in impure forms."

It is important to understand this responsiveness without judgments, in order to understand the unique method of dzogchen, self-liberation. The famous nineteenth-century dzogchen master dPal-sprul Rinpoche explained self-liberation concretely and precisely:

> (The practitioner of self-liberation) is like an ordinary person as far as the way in which the thoughts of pleasure and pain, hope and fear, manifest themselves as this creative energy. However, the ordinary person, taking these really seriously and judging them as acceptable or rejecting them, continues to get caught up in situations and becomes conditioned by attachment and aversion. Not doing this, a practitioner, when such thoughts arise, experiences freedom (in either of three ways): initially, by recognizing the thought for what it is, it is freed just like meeting a previous acquaintance; then it is freed in and of itself, like a snake shedding its skin; and finally, thought is freed in being unable to be of benefit or harm, like a thief entering an empty house.[72]

Many people spend years believing they are practicing dzogchen, while they are actually practicing calming or insight meditation. Freeing or liberating thought does not mean ignoring, letting go of, being indifferent to, observing, or even not having thoughts. It means being present in hope and fear, pain and pleasure, not as objects before us, but as the radiant clarity of our natural state. Thus anger, for example, when experienced dualistically, is an irritation which we may indulge in or reject, depending on our conditioning. Either way we are caught up in it and act out of it. But when aware of anger as a manifestation of clarity, its energy is a very fresh aware-

---

72. *khas pa 'sri rgyal po'i khyad chos*, ms, n.p., n.d., p. 10b-11a.

ness of the particulars of the situation. However, these particulars are
no longer irritating.

What the state of pure and total presence (*byang chub sems*) is,
how to find it, and how to continue with it, are the subjects discussed by Longchenpa, the greatest philosopher-mystic of this ancient teaching.

APPENDIX A

The History and Structure of the kun byed rgyal po

by Namkhai Norbu

In the middle period of Tibetan buddhism,[73] clever scholars and intellectuals such as 'Bri-gung dpal-'dzin (1143–1217), not understanding its profound and esoteric real meaning, negated the way in which the valuable dzogchen teaching set forth its outlook, practice, behavior, and goal. They also claimed that its fundamental texts, such as the *kun byed rgyal po*, were fabrications by Tibetan scholars. These abysmally wrong-headed ideas were completely cleared up in the works of great scholars and practitioners such as Klong-chen rab-'byams-pa (1308–1364), Sog zlog-pa blo-gros rgyal-mtshan (1552-?) and dPa'-bo gtsug-lag phreng-ba (1454-?). Let us take some examples from Sog zlog-pa's refutation of 'Bri-gung dpal-'dzin in his *Dragon's Roar of the Real Meaning:*

---

73. In Tibet the authenticity of the *kun byed rgyal po* was questioned. For Western scholarship bearing on this text, see Samten Karmay, "A Discussion on the Doctrinal Position of the rDzogs-chen from the 10th to the 13th Centuries," in *Journal Asiatique*, fasc. 1 & 2, 1975, 147–155; Eva Dargyay, "The Concept of a 'Creator God' in Tantric Buddhism," *Journal of the International Association of Buddhist Studies*, v. 8, no. 1, 31–47; "A Nyingma Text: The Kun byed rgyal po'i mdo," in B. Aziz and M. Kapstein, eds., *Soundings in Tibetan Civilization* (New Delhi: Manohar Pub., 1985); David Germano, "Architecture and Absense in the Secret Tantric History of the Great Perfection" (*rdzog chen*), *Journal of the International Association of Buddhist Studies*, v. 17, no. 2, 203–335, esp. 234 ff.

['Bri-gung dpal-'dzin stated that] Nyang-ston smra-ba'i seng-ge
wrote the eighteen 'mother and son' texts of the *sems sde*,[74] [and
Sog zlog-pa replied that] although the *kun byed rgyal po* belongs
to the [dzogchen teaching of] primordial mind, it is not among
these eighteen texts of the *sems sde*.[75]

['Bri-gung dpal-'dzin stated that] in the practice of the *kun
byed rgyal po*, all types of gazes, bodily positions, and methods
for controlling the body's energy were rejected; all common ac-
tivities, even impure ones, were understood to be in the sphere
of absolute reality, so that one enacts the absolute in everything
one does; accustoming oneself to this, one eliminates obstacles
so that all faults become positive qualities; and just hearing these
instructions makes one an Awakened One.

[Sog zlog-pa replied that] in relaxing into one's natural
condition, which is mahāmudrā, nothing need be done by
way of bodily position or gazes; in the "Ganges' Instructions
on Mahāmudrā,"[76] Tilopa said that one does not become an
Awakened One by contrived actions and that by meditating one
doesn't see the truth of non-meditation. Also the lord of yogis,
Virupa, in his dohās,[77] says that not renouncing or accomplishing or holding on to anything, but doing whatever one pleases
without being blocked, is the supreme, most noble way of behaving. The arrow-like Mahāmudrā instructions of the great
master of mTshal to De'u-ri ras-pa make the same point.[78] The
statement that if one understands impure actions to be absolute
reality, then all faults become positive qualities, should make

---

74. See *Primordial Experience*, pp. 7–9.

75. *nges pa'i don gyi 'brug sgra*, in *Collected Writings of Sog zlog pa blos gros
rgyal mtshan*, v. 1 (New Delhi: 1975). Hereafter N.

76. See *gDams ngag mdzod*, v. 5 (New Delhi: 1971), pp. 33–36. These are the
famous mahāmudrā instructions of Tilopa to Naropa.

77. Virupa's dohās can be found in the collection *Doha mdzod brgyad* (Rumtek,
Sikkim: 1972) and his hagiography in Keith Dowman, *Masters of Mahamudra* (State
University of New York Press, 1985), pp. 43–52.

78. This is Zhang 'Gro-ba'i mgon-po (1123–1193), who is discussed in
Roerich, trans., *The Blue Annals* (Calcutta: Motilal Banarsidass, 1953), pp. 711–15.
This bKa' brgyud pa master founded the monastery of mTshal in 1175.

you recall the verse of the *Hevajra Tantra*, 'Just as dirt is cleaned by dirt, the passions are purified by the passions.'[79]

Further, in the Edict of Pho-brang Zhi-ba 'Od, the nephew of the King of Pu-hrangs, Lha Bla-ma Ye-shes 'Od, there is the refutation, as quoted by Sog zlog-pa:

> The eighteen tantras of the *sems sde*,[80] written by Drang-nga shag-tshul at the Copper Glacier in Upper Nyang, such as the *kun byed rgyal po*, the ten esoteric sutras,[81] the *ye shes gsang ba*,[82] commentaries, outlines, initiation and meditation instructions, instructions on psychic phenomena, the *srid pa'i rgyud*, as well as all the teachings on the *ma mo*, such as the *ma mo tantras*,[83] and finally the 'Five Kingly Teachings': the innumerable tantras, commentaries, instructions, and practical handbooks [associated with these, are prohibited].[84]

In reply to this Sog zlog-pa states:

> In regard to the statement that Drang-nga shag-tshul wrote the eighteen texts of the *sems sde*, such as the *kun byed rgyal po*, the ten esoteric sutras, and the *ye shes gsang ba*, this does not refer to the [actual] eighteen texts of *sems sde*: the five early translations of Vairocana and the thirteen later ones of Vimalamitra.[85] The five early translations of Vairocana are: *nam mkha che, rtsal chen yang dag drug pa, rig pa'i ku byug, sku la 'jug pa,* and *rdzogs pa spyi gcod.*[86] Some people replace the last two with the *kyung chen lding ba* and the *sgom don drug pa*. The *kun byed rgyal po*, the ten

---

79. N., 325.

80. See *Primordial Experience*, pp 7–9.

81. K., no. 2.

82. K., no. 56.

83. The tantras are found in vols. 30, 31 of the *rNying ma rgyud 'bum*.

84. N., 464.

85. See *Primordial Experience*, pp. 7–9.

86. *ibid.*

sutras, and the *ye shes gsang ba* do not belong to these eighteen *sems sde* texts. Because 'Bri-gung dpal-'dzin does not even make this distinction, he can't see the target his arrow is headed for. Not only that, but there is no agreement among those who make such statements. 'Gos lha-btsas says that the thirteen later texts, such as the *rmad byung*, were written by Sang-rgyas ye-shes,[87] but this is refuted merely by saying that they were translations by Vimalamitra. As to Drang-nga shag-tshul writing the *kun byed rgyal po*, others say it was written by Vairocana; while still others say it was the *gsang ba'i snying po*[88] which Vairocana wrote. These assertions are without foundation.[89]

The reality of the matter is given by dPa-bo gtsug-lag phreng-ba in his *mkhas pa'i dga' ston*:

> How could genuine tantras such as those of the mahāyoga, anuyoga, and atiyoga be fabrications by philosophers, rationalists, and the like? Because these are not within the realm of comprehension of even the śrāvakas and pratyekabuddhas, then how much more so would this be in the case of others like the philosophers? If someone thinks these texts were spoken by an Awakened One other than the Teacher (Śākyamuni), then in that case they have been established as canonical.[90]

The Omniscient One among the 'Brug-pa, Padma dKar-po, in his *chos 'byung bstan pa'i padma rgyas pa'i nyin byed*, stated:

> In the instructions known as dzogchen there are the *sems sde*, *klong sde*, and *man ngag sde*. The *sems sde* consists of the five [early translations] by Vairocana and the thirteen [later ones] by Vimalamitra. The *klong sde* stems from Vairocana, while the *man ngag sde*, also known as the *snying thig*, comes from Vimalamitra.

---

87. gNubs-chen Sang-rgyas ye-shes, disciple of Padmasambhava, and author of the *bsam gtan mig sgron*.

88. This is the tantra referred to above on p. 49, n. 55.

89. N., 469.

90. Satapitaka Series, v. 9 (New Delhi, 1959), p. 182.

The lineage of the latter's student, Myang Ting-'dzin bzang-po, spread it in Tibet. Then from rMa Rin-chen mchog, sNyags Jñānakumāra, and sNubs Sangs-rgyas ye-shes spread the greater part of the canonical teachings; from this came the statement of 'Gos Lotsawa that the three inner divisions of teachings of the old tradition were fabrications.[91]

Excellent and impartial scholars and practitioners, possessing both experience and a thorough grasp of the subject, recognize that the *kun byed rgyal po* is an absolutely fundamental ancient text of dzogchen, which reveals the profound, hidden dimension of reality. Therefore, in the tantra section of the Beijing edition of the Canon; in the thirty-volume *rnying ma'i rgyud 'bum* compiled by disciples of 'Gro-mgon nam-mkha dpal (1170–1236), himself the son of mNga-bdag nyang-ral nyi-ma'i 'od-zer (1124–1192), on the basis of 'Gro-mgon's *rgyud 'bum* written in gold; and in Zur 'ug-pa's rough edition, the text is to be found. However, gTer-chen Ratna gling-pa did not include it among the translations of tantras from the early period, because he applied the strict criterion of it not being found among the inner tantras in the *lDan dkar ma Catalog.*[92] After this period, texts were collected from all quarters to compile a new *rnying ma'i rgyud 'bum*, and sMin-gling gter-chen 'Gyur-med rdo-rje (1646–1714) had a new edition made in silver and gold in 1686. An edition was compiled by gCung-chos dpal bzang-po (1654–1717), but Kun-mkhyen 'Jigs-med gling-pa (1729–98) made sMin-gling's edition the basis of his work, compiling a new edition with twenty-five additional volumes. 'Jigs-med gling-pa also wrote his "'Ornament which Encompasses the Whole of Jambudvīpa,' True Information about the Precious Collection of Ancient Tantras."[93] Based on these the sDe-dge edition was printed. In Bhutan, in the 16th century, through Kah-thog-pa bSod-nams rgyal-mtshan, and then in the 17th century, at mTshams-brag monastery, a forty-six-volume edition was compiled.[94] In all the above-mentioned editions, the *kun byed rgyal*

91. Satapitaka Series, v. 75, (New Delhi, 1968), p. 390.

92. This is a catalog of translations from the early period of Tibetan buddhism.

93. K., no. 407.

94. See above n. 11.

po, which is like the root of all the tantras, agamas, and upadeśas of ati dzogchen, is clearly evident.

Although there appear to be many variations in the texts of the *kun byed rgyal po*, there are no substantial differences in actual meaning. The end of Chapter 57 of this work reads, "The sutra agama in 57 (chapters)."[95] Then, the twelve chapters up to 69 are called the "sutra agama in 12 (chapters)" or the "appended tantra;"[96] while the next chapters up to 84 are called the "second appended tantra," or all the chapters from 58 to 84 are called the "appended tantra." Thus, there are only slight differences in terminology, as there are in the various redactions of the translators' colophons.

If we here compare the Beijing, mTshams-brag, and *Vairocana rGyud 'bum* editions, we find the Beijing and mTshams-brag with identical titles:

> In Sanskrit: *Sarvadharmamahāśāntibodhicittakulayarāja*
> In Tibetan: *chos thams cad rdzogs pa chen po byang chub kyi sems kun byed rgyal po*
> The Supreme Ordering Principle in the Universe, the State of Total Completeness in which Everything Comes to Full Presence[97]

The end of the 57th chapter in the Beijing edition says:

> (The Tantra of) The Supreme Ordering Principle in the Universe, the State of Pure and Total Presence, is completed, translated upon request by the Indian scholar Śrī Saṃhaprabha and the Tibetan translator Pa-gor Vairocana.[98]

while the mTshams-brag edition has:

> The Chapter which Sets Forth the Teaching, from (the Tantra of) the Supreme Ordering Principle in the Universe, the State of

---

95. T., 192.

96. B., 122,2,2; T., 225.

97. B., 93,1,1; T., 2; The *Vairocana rgyud 'bum* (Leh, Ladakh: 1971), v. 1, 383. Hereafter V.

98. B., 118,5,2,2–3.

Pure and Total Presence, the Sutra Agama in 57 (Chapters). It is hereby completed.[99]

Then, a little more than three pages further on, at the end of an explanation of the 57 Sutra Agamas, it says:

The explanation of the 57 Sutra Agamas attached to the ['Tantra of] the Supreme Ordering Principle in the Universe.'[100]

At the end of the 69th chapter, the Beijing and the mTshams-brag editions state:

The 12 Sutra Agamas called the 'Appended Tantra' are herein completed.[101]

The colophons of the Beijing and mTshams-brag editions both state:

A Tantra about the State of Pure and Total Presence, the Supreme Ordering Principle in the Universe, Whose Point of View, like Space, has No Center or Periphery. The Eighty-four supremely esoteric sutra agamas whose supreme meaning is the power of space, are hereby completed.[102]

The translators' colophon of the Beijing edition states:

Translated upon request by the Indian scholar dPal-gyi Seng-ge mGon-po and the Bhikshu Vairocana,[103]

while the mTshams-brag has:

Translated upon request by the Indian scholar dPal-gyi Seng-ge and the Bhikshu Vairocana.[104]

---

99. T., 192,4–5.
100. T., 199,4.
101. B., 122,2,2; T., 225,4–5.
102. B., 165,5,1; T., 261,6.
103. B., 126,5,2.
104. T., 261,7.

The *Vairocana rgyud 'bum* edition begins:

> Herein is contained A Tantra about the State of Pure and Total
> Presence, the Supreme Ordering Principle in the Universe,
> whose Point of View, like Space, has No Center or Periphery.
> The 84 Excellent Esoteric Sutra Agamas whose Significance is
> like the Power of Space.[105]

So, the main body of the work is the 57 chapters or sutra agamas,
after which, in the Beijing and mTshams-brag editions, there is the
"Appended Tantra" that begins:

> The Supreme Organizing Principle in the Universe, the State
> of Pure and Total Presence, having thoroughly grasped un-
> originated, self-generating primordial awareness, did not say
> anything.[106]

The two editions correspond right to the end of the 84 Sutra Agamas. At the conclusion of Chapter 69 they both read:

> The twelve Sutra Agamas called the 'Appended Tantra' are
> completed.[107]

While there is no final colophon to the text of the *kun byed rgyal po*
found in the *Vairocana rgyud 'bum*, the end of the 84th Sutra Agama
reads the same. The translators' colophon states:

> Translated upon request by the Indian scholar Śrī Siṃhakala
> and the Tibetan translator, Bhikshu Vairocana.[108]

At the end of the main body of the *kun byed rgyal po* it says,

---

105. V., 383.
106. B., 118,5,4; T., 225,4.
107. B., 122,2,2; T., 225,4.
108. V., 435,6.

The Tantra whose Perspective is without Center or Periphery, like Space.[109]

Indeed these 57 sutra agamas clearly present the perspective of total completeness, which is totally beyond limitations such as center or periphery, like space.

Translated and annotated by Kennard Lipman

---

109. B., 125,5,1; T., 261,6.

APPENDIX B

*Quotations from the Root Text**

Quote Starting on Page	Root Text Chapter : Page . Line	Quote Starting on Page	Root Text Chapter : Page . Line
20a	33 : 117.5	33b	sde gde bstan 'gyur
20b	64 : 213.1		dbu ma, vol. sa 3a.2
20c	59 : 142.3	34a	22 : 89.6
21	38 : 129.2	34b	9 : 41.3
22a	59 : 202.4	36a	32 : 113.6
22b	84 : 261.2	36b	80 : 248.1
23a	79 : 246.5	36c	73 : 234.3
23b	12 : 58.4	37a	73 : 233.6
24a	27 : 99.7	37b	70 : 227.3
24b	27 : 99.6	37c	25 : 93.7
25	83 : 256.6	39a	7 : 30.2
26a	83 : 257.1	40a	66 : 218.2
26b	83 : 257.4	40b	30 : 108.2
27	13 : 61.5	41	26 : 98.1
29	22 : 89.4	42	27 : 97.6
32a	6 : 25.5	43a	30 : 111.2
32b	6 : 22.5	43b	74 : 235.3
33a	15 : 71.7	44a	52 : 176.3

*The references, except where noted, are to *The mtshams-brag manuscript* of the rñing ma rgyud 'bum, Vol. 1, Thimpu: The Royal Government of Bhutan, 1982

Quote Starting on Page	*Root Text Chapter:Page.Line*	*Quote Starting on Page*	*Root Text Chapter:Page.Line*
44b	66:217.4	48b	49:167.2
45	78:244.3	49	67:220.4
46	78:245.2	50a	68:223.1
47	42:141.2	50b	80:248.1
48a	49:165.4	53	83:258.2

Glossary of Tibetan Terms

kun byed (rgyal po)	universal creativity, supreme ordering principle of the universe, creative energy of the universe, majestic creativity within everything, that which fashions everything, universal creativity that makes everything possible
klong	expanse
sku	dimension
dgongs pa	deep experience, deepest sense, primordial condition, deep structure
ngang	ongoing state, dimension, condition, state
ngang dvangs	ongoing lucidity
ngo bo	essence, being
chos	events and meanings, phenomena, what is experienced
chos sku	embodying wholeness, dimension of being, fundamental dimension of reality
chos nyid	the actual state of things, reality, state of being
chos dbyings	field of all events and meanings, reality field
mnyams bzhag	state of contemplation
syning po	quintessence, inner reality, core
lta ba	perspective, vision, point of view
stong pa	open dimensional, open, empty
stong pa nyid	openness, emptiness, voidness, void

theg pa	spiritual pursuit, approach to the teaching
thugs	awareness, primordial state
thugs rje	responsiveness, felt reality, energy, resonance
thog 'bebs	direct entry into understanding
de bzhin nyid	reality
don	reality, significance, meaning, benefit, truth, message
rnal byor	tuning in
rnal bzhag chen po	great naturalness
snang ba	what appears, experience, that which is experienced
sprul sku	dimension of apparitional being
spros bral	freedom from constructing
phun sum tshogs pa	excellencies
byang chub	pure and total presence
byang chub kyi sems	pure and total presence, state of pure and total presence
dbyings	field, reality field
rdzogs chen	total completeness, great perfection, absolute perfection, total natural perfection
ma skye (skye med)	unborn, never becomes what it seems to be
zang thal	unobstructed
yangs pa	vast expanse
ye nas	primordial, primary
ye shes	pristine awareness, ever-fresh awareness
rang gi ngo bo	the content of what one is, what it is in itself
rang grol	intrinsic freedom, self-liberation
rang byung ye shes	self-refreshing awareness, self-generating pristine awareness
rang bzhin	nature, actuality, frame of reference
rang shar	self-originating
rig pa	pure presence, awareness, sheer presence
rol pa	play, play of experience
longs spyod rdzogs sku	dimension of the full richness of being
lhun sgrub	spontaneously present, spontaneously perfect
lhun rdzogs	spontaneously complete
sa	level, stage, plateau
sangs rgyas	buddha, one who wakes up to what is, awakened one

sems rgyud	primordial state
sems nyid	mind itself, the pure fact of awareness
gsang ba	hidden
gsung	communication, symphony
ati yoga	primordial yoga

Further Readings

Bdud-'joms-gling-pa, Gter-ston. *Buddhahood Without Meditation: A Visionary Account Known as Refining Apparent Phenomena* (Nang Jang). Junction City, CA: Padma, 1994.

Bdud-'joms 'Jigs-bral-ye-shes-rdo-rje. *The Nyingma School of Tibetan Buddhism: Its Fundamentals and History* (bstan-pa'i rnam-gzhag' and 'chos-byung). Boston: Wisdom, 1991.

Dargyay, Eva M. *The Rise of Esoteric Buddhism in Tibet.* Delhi: Motilal Banarsidass, 1977.

Dowman, Keith. *The Flight of the Garuda.* Boston: Wisdom, 1994.

Garab Dorje. *The Golden Letters* (tshig gsum gnad brdeg). Translated by John Myrdhin Reynolds. Foreword by Namkhai Norbu Rinpoche. Ithaca, NY: Snow Lion, 1996.

Guenther, Herbert V. "Absolute Perfection" in *Crystal Mirror I.* Berkeley: Dharma Publishing, n.d. (1971).

——————. *Buddhist Philosophy in Theory and Practice.* Berkeley: Shambala, 1971.

——————. *From Reductionism to Creativity: rDzogs-chen and the New Sciences of Mind.* Boston: Shambhala, 1989.

——————. *Matrix of Mystery.* Boulder: Shambhala, 1984.

——————. *Meditation Differently.* Delhi: Motilal Banarsidass, 1992.

—————————. *The Teachings of Padmasambhava.* Leiden: E.J. Brill, 1996.

—————————. *Wholeness Lost and Wholeness Regained: Forgotten Tales of Individuation from Ancient Tibet.* Albany, NY: SUNY, 1994.

Jigme Lingpa. "Nying Tig *or the Innermost Essence" (snying thig sgom pa'i bya bral gyi gol shor tshar gcig senge'i nga ro)* in *Mudra.* Translated by Chogyam Trungpa. Berkeley: Shambhala, 1972.

Karmay, Samten Gyaltsen. *The Great Perfection.* Leiden: E.J. Brill, 1988.

Klong-chen-pa Dri-med-'od-zer. *Buddha Mind: An Anthology of Longchen Rabjam's Writings on Dzogpa Chenpo.* Translated by Tulku Thondup, Ithaca, NY: Snow Lion, 1989.

—————————. *The Four-Themed Precious Garland: An Introduction to Dzog Chen (chos bzhi rin po che 'phreng ba).* Translated by Alexander Berzin, Sherpa Tulku, and Mathew Kapstein. Dharamsala: Library of Tibetan Works and Archives, 1979.

—————————. *Kindly Bent to Ease Us (ngal gso skor gsum).* Translated by Herbert V. Guenther in 3 volumes. Emeryville: Dharma Publishing 1975–76.

—————————. "The Natural Freedom of Mind" *(sems nyid rang grol)* in *Crystal Mirror IV.* Translated by Herbert V. Guenther. Emeryville: Dharma Publishing, 1975.

—————————. *The Precious Treasury of the Way of Abiding and The Exposition of the Quintessential Meaning of the Three Categories: A Commentary on the Precious Treasury of the Way of Abiding.* Junction City, CA: Padma, 1998.

Kong-sprul Blo-gros-mtha'-yas. *Myriad Worlds: Buddhist Cosmology in Abhidharma, Kalacakra and Dzog-chen* (Chapter 1 of Shes bya mtha' yas pa'i rgya mtsho). Ithaca, NY: Snow Lion, 1995.

Low, James. *Simply Being: Texts in the Dzogchen Tradition.* London: Vajra Press, 1998.

Mañjuśrīmitra. *Primordial Experience: An Introduction to rDzogs Chen Meditation.* Translated by Namkhai Norbu and Kennard Lipman with Barrie Simmons. Boston: Shambhala, 1987.

Namkhai Norbu. *The Crystal and the Way of Light.* John Shane, ed. London: Routledge & Kegan-Paul, 1986.

—————————. *The Cycle of Day and Night, Where One Proceeds Along the Path of the Primordial Yoga.* Translated and edited by John M. Reynolds. Oakland: Zhang Zhung Editions, 1984. 2d Ed. Barrytown, NY: Station Hill Press, 1987.

—————————. *Dzogchen: The Self-Perfected State.* Edited by Adriano Clemente, translated by John Shane. Ithaca, NY: Snow Lion, 1996.

—————————. *The Mirror: Advice on the Presence of Awareness.* Barrytown, NY: Station Hill, 1996.

—————————. *Rigbai Kujyug: The Six Vajra Verses.* Singapore: Rinchen, 1990.

Neumaier-Dargyay, E.K. *The Sovereign All-Creating Mind: The Motherly Buddha.* Albany, NY: SUNY, 1992.

Nyoshul Khenpo, Rinpoche. *Natural Great Perfection: Dzogchen Teachings and Vajra Songs.* Ithaca, NY: Snow Lion, 1995.

Padmasambhava. (*rig-pa ngo sprod gcer-mthong rang-grol,* rediscovered by Karma gling-pa) Translated three times in: W.Y. Evans-Wentz, *The Tibetan Book of the Great Liberation.* London: Oxford University Press, 1954; Karma gling-pa. *Self-Liberation through Seeing with Naked Awareness.* Translated by John Myrdhim Reynolds. Barrytown, NY: Station Hill, 1989; and *The Tibetan Book of the Dead.* Translated by Robert A.F. Thurman. New York: Bantan, 1994.

Paltrul Rinpoche. *The Three Incisive Precepts of Garab Dorje; the Dzokchen Precepts of the Extraordinary Reality of the Glorious Sovereign Wisdom of Patrul Rimpoche; Patrul Rimpoche's Short Elucidation of the mKhas-pa Sri rGyal-po.* Translated by Keith Dowman. Kathmandu: Diamond Sow, n.d.

—————————. *Lion's Gaze: A Commentary on Tsig Sum Nedek (tshig gsum gnad brdeg* and *mkhas-pa shri rgyal-po'i khyad-chos 'grel-ba dang bcas-pa)* by Khenchen Palden Sherab Rinpoche and Khenpo Tsewang Dongyal Rinpoche, translated by Sarah Harding. Boca Raton, FL: Sky Dancer Press, 1998.

Sogyal Rinpoche. *Dzogchen and Padmasambhava,* 2d Ed. [Santa Cruz, CA]: Rigpa Fellowship, 1990.

Index

absolute completeness, 13
absolute perfection, 13
absolute reality, 80
acceptance and rejection, 15, 42, 44,
    49, 66, 77
actuality, 75
affirmation, 28, 44
after death experience, 62
agama, 4, 5, 6
anger, 40, 77
antidote, 44, 46, 60, 66
anuyoga, 2, 5, 6, 82
anxiety, 46, 50
apparitional being, dimension of, 7,
    20, 31
appearance, 15, 32, 35, 39, 41, 42, 44,
    74
  and openness, unity of, 42
appended tantra, 2, 84
approach, to the teachings, 20–23, 57,
    65. *See also* path.
  causal, 50, 69
  dzogchen, 61
  .superiority of, 72
appropriate action, path of, 3
archetype, 30, 65
  energy, 62

forms, 27
of the Self, 62, 63, 64
symbols, 67
vision, 68
atiyoga, 2, 4, 5, 13, 82
attachment, 34, 40, 41, 67, 77
audience, 74
autonomy, 63
aversion, 41, 42, 45, 67, 77
Awakened One, 20. *See also* Buddha.
awareness, 69
  all-accomplishing, 42
  brilliant, 15
  discriminating, 42
  ever-fresh, 15, 19, 28, 33, 66, 68
  fact of, 28
  fresh, 77
  inner reality of, 43
  mirror-like, 42
  non-dualistic, 41
  of utter sameness, 42
  primordial, 4, 70
  pristine, 38, 42, 44, 48, 72
  pure, 75
  pure fact of, 19, 33, 35, 48, 54, 57,
    65, 75
  reality-field's, 42

awareness (*continued*)
  self-arising pristine, 35, 49
  self-refreshing, 15, 21, 52, 73, 74
  sensory, 14

basis, 66. *See also* ground.
behavior, 2, 44. *See also* way of life.
being-for-others, 34
bindu, 71
blessing, 62, 64
bliss, 36
  and openness, unity of, 42
bodhicitta, 2, 6, 69, 70, 75
  absolute, 70
  according to dzogchen, 71, 73
  according to tantra, 71
  realization of, 72
  relative, 69, 70
  ultimate, 69
bodhisattva, 5, 42, 72
body, 4, 67
  according to sutra, 67
  according to tantra, 67
branch tantra, 2
'Bri-gung dpal-'dzin, 79, 82
bsam gtan mig sgron, 82
buddha, 47, 50, 57, 76
  Śākyamuni, 4, 21, 67, 82
  qualities, 76
buddhahood, 4, 31, 40, 72
  state of, 39
buddhas, 32, 35, 38, 44
  five, 8, 27, 28, 30, 38
  of the three times, 65
buddhism, 58, 69
  knowledge about, 61
buddhist, definition of, 3
byang chub sems, 2
byin rlabs, 62

calmness, practice of, 66
capabilities, 75, 76
capacity, 2, 32, 69
career, 21. *See also* approach.

cause and effect, 33, 49, 50, 66
cessation of suffering, 67
channels, 66, 70
charismatic activity, 2, 4, 35
*chos 'byung bstan pa'i padma rgyas pa'i
  nyin byed,* 82
Chos-rje kun-dga' don-grub, 28
clarity, 51
  and openness, unity of, 42
clear expanse, 15, 52
clear light, 15, 33, 55
  self-originating, 36
cognitive responsiveness, 7, 28
commitment, 2, 4, 25
communication, 43
compassion, 20, 25, 29, 31, 34, 54,
    69, 70
  contrasted with love, 72
  half-baked, 54
  in dzogchen, 71
  lack of, 51
completion stage, 3
conceptualization, 33, 50
conditioning, 77
constituents, psychological, 34
contemplation, 1, 7, 37, 48
  levels of, 52
creative intelligence, intention of, 65
creative energy of the universe, 23
creative intelligence, 20, 39, 74
creativity, 46, 75
  universal, 14, 19 ff., 57
cultivation, 8
culture, 58, 61

Dalai Lama, Fifth, 13
De'u-ri ras-pa, 80
depth psychology, 27, 62
desire, 14, 40, 42, 45
desireless lotus, 48
development stage, 3, 69
dGa'-rab rdo-rje, 7, 8, 27, 28, 53, 59

Dhammapada, 21
dharmakāya, 27, 30. *See also* dimension of being.
dimension(s)
  of apparitional being, 47
  of being, 7, 20, 27, 47, 52
  of reality, 36
  three, 7, 20, 50, 52, 65, 67
  unborn, 37
direct introduction, 62
discipline, 58
dkyil 'khor bsgom, 70
dPa'-bo gtsug-lag phreng-ba, 79, 82
Dragon's Roar of the Real Meaning, 79
Drang-nga shag-tshul, 81, 82
dream(s), 33, 41, 52
  lucid, 52
Drung ye-shes dbang-po, 28
dualism, 32, 60, 74, 77
duality, 33, 35
'dus pa'i mdo, 2, 28
dzogchen, 2, 6, 13, 16, 57, 60, 62, 64,
  69, 71, 76, 83
  agama, 2
  implementation of, 59
  method of, 75
  method of liberating passions, 72
  path of, 61, 65, 66
  teaching, 79

Edict of Pho-brang Zhi-ba 'Od, 81
ego, 64
  deflation, 63
  inflation, 63
elements, 37, 38, 39. *See also* matter.
emptiness, meditation on, 36
empty, 76. *See also* openness.
energy, 76
  as basis of tantric path, 66
  centers, 70
  foci, 66
  primordial, 5
enlightenment, 65, 69
entities, 42

environment, 32, 35, 44, 67, 73, 74
envy, 41, 42
essence, 75
events and meanings, 50, 51
  total field of, 72
excellencies, 39, 40
existence, 35, 58
experience, 11 ff., 19, 32 ff., 60, 69, 70,
  75
  consensual, 67
  details of, 49
  direct, 54, 57, 65
  primordial, 58
  process of, 76
  pure fact of, 15
  sense-based, 66
  total field of, 28
explanatory tantra, 2

facets of existence, three, 4
fear, 44, 46, 49, 51, 52, 63, 77
female principle, 71
field of reality, 28
'Five Kingly Teachings', 81
focus, 11, 14, 36
forces, archetypal, 63
form, 32, 38, 41, 43, 44
  apparitional, 5
four noble truths, 21
frame of reference, 23
frustration, 44, 67
  and suffering, 3

g·Yu-gra snying-po, 28
gCung-chos dpal bzang-po, 83
gNubs-chen Sang-rgyas ye-shes, 82
goal, 4, 57, 65, 66
'Gos lha-btsas, 82
'Gos Lotsawa, 83
great perfection, 13
great wheel of letters, 48
'Gro-mgon nam-mkha dpal, 83
ground, 4, 28, 75. *See also* basis.
gsang ba'i snying po, 2, 82

gSar-ma, 70
gter ma, 27
gTer-chen Ratna gling-pa, 83
guru, 63, 64
guruyoga, 29 ff., 62, 63, 64, 65

happiness, 44, 54
health, 44, 60
heritage, 27
hidden treasure teachings, 27
hope, 15, 46, 49, 51, 52, 54, 77

illusion, 41
impermanence, 3, 51
impressive encounter (mudra), 3
independent, those who are content
    with being, 42, 72
indestructible comprehension, 48
indirect teaching, 20
individuality, 64
inhabitants, 35, 44, 73, 74
initiation, 2, 4, 66
    tantric, 62
inner heat, 71
insight, practice of, 66
integrated structure (mandala), 43, 44,
    48
integration, 61
intellect, 66
intelligence of the universe, 23
intense display, 48
intermediate state, 55
interpretive guidelines, four, 6
intrinsic clarity, 37
intrinsic freedom, 4, 5, 57, 60, 69, 71,
    75. See also self-liberation
    path of, 4

'Jam-dbyangs mkhyen-brtse'i dbang-
    po, 13
'Jam-dbyangs kun-dga' rgyal-mtshan,
    29
'Jigs-med gling-pa, 83
journey, spiritual, 16

judgment, 77
    absence of, 51
Jung, Carl, 27, 62, 63

Kah-thog-pa bSod-nams rgyal-mtshan,
    83
karma, 15, 41, 51, 55
Karmapa, 13
klong chen rab 'byams rgyal po'i rgyud, 3
klong sde, 2, 3, 82
Klong-chen rab-'byams-pa. See
    Longchenpa.
kun byed rgyal po, 73, 74
kun byed rgyal po (text), 1, 4, 13, 28,
    79–87
kyung chen lding ba, 81

lCe dga'-ba'i dbang-po, 28
lCog-ro skyes-bzang legs-smin, 28
lDan dkar ma Catalog, 83
Lha Bla-ma Ye-shes 'Od, 81
lha'i nga rgyal, 69
life-energy, 63
life-forms, 32, 45
life-process, 66
light everywhere, level of, 48
lineage, 27
listening and preaching, those who are
    content with, 21, 42. See also
    śrāvakas.
Longchenpa, 7, 28, 79
love, 25, 44, 72

Ma mo tantras, 81
mahāmudrā, 80
mahāsaṃdhi, 13
mahāyāna, 21
mahāyoga, 2, 5, 82
majestic creative intelligence, 43
majestic creativity, 23, 36, 37
    child of, 49
majestic pure presence, 42
male principle, 71
man ngag sde, 2, 3, 82

mandala, 2, 4, 40, 62, 66, 67, 69, 70, 71, 74
  expressive energy of, 68
  of mind, 68
  universe-as-, 74
manifestation, 32
Mañjuśrīmitra, 28
mantra, 2, 4, 5, 68, 69
mantrayāna, 2, 3, 6
master, 63
master-disciple relationship, 62
mastery, 63
material dimension, 28
material world, 14
materialism, spiritual, 11
matter, states of, 33
mdo, 2
meaning of life, 54, 57
meaningfulness of being, 68
meditation, 2, 4, 29, 35, 37, 46, 50, 51, 52, 61
  body as support of, 67
  calming, 68, 77
  insight, 68, 77
meditation posture, seven point, 35
mental activity, 37
mental event, 33, 75
merit, accumulation of, 60
method, 65, 68
mind, 4, 33, 37, 47, 54, 57, 67, 74, 76
  in buddhism, 68
  primordial, 5
  samsaric, 75,
mirror, 74, 75, 76
mkhas pa'i dga' ston, 82
mNga-bdag nyang-ral nyi-ma'i 'od-zer, 83
mTshugs-med chos-rje rin-po-che raja, 29
mTshur-mchog-gi bla-ma, 28
mudras, four, 3
mundane world, 70
Myang Ting-'dzin bzang-po, 83

nam mkha che, 81
natural condition, 28
natural light, 52
natural state, 16, 57, 60, 61, 62, 63, 65, 69, 71, 72, 74, 75
  energy of, 76
  introduction to, 59
  radiant clarity of, 77
  realization of, 72
nature of mind, 1, 44, 45
negation, 28, 44
Ngag-bdang blo-bzang rgya-mtsho, 13
nirmāṇakāya, 4, 27
nirvana, 3, 21, 50, 75
non-conceptuality, 38
non-differentiation, level of, 49
non-duality, 15, 42, 44
non-meditation, 80
non-perfection, 50
non-virtue, 44
nondivisiveness, state of, 38
nondual nature, 28
nonessentiality, 3
Nyang-ston smra-ba'i seng-ge, 80
nyingma, 2, 5, 13

obstacles, 8, 21, 35, 59, 60, 61, 80
  clarification of, 66
  elimination of, 66
ocean replete with qualities, 5
old tradition. *See* nyingma.
ongoing lucidity, 36
openness, 3, 11, 21, 51, 61, 76
  and appearance, unity of, 42
  and bliss, unity of, 42
  and clarity, unity of, 42
  and pure presence, unity of, 42
  direct understanding of, 69
  feeling of, 70
  of being, 70
oral explanation, 25, 26
oral instruction, 50
ornaments, 40, 41, 42
outlook, 3, 4. *See also* perspective

pāramitāyāna, 6
Padma dKar-po, 13, 82
Padmasambhava, 12, 82
pain, 63, 77
Pali Canon, 21
passions, 14, 41, 49, 61, 72, 81
  intrinsic freedom of, 40
  playing out of, 70
  refining away, 42, 72
  self liberation of, 72
  transformation of, 42, 67
path(s), 3, 4, 42, 44, 48, 57, 61, 66
  as goal, 66
  different, 65
  dzogchen, 62, 64, 65, 66
  following a, 68
  goal-directed, 70
  gradual, 20, 61, 66, 70
  of renunciation, 66
  of self-liberation, 66
  of transformation, 66
  superiority of, 65
  sutric, 66, 67
  to traverse, 35
  tantric, 64, 66
perfection, 39, 50
person, 64
personality, 64
  cult, 63
perspective, 7, 8, 32 ff., 35, 50, 52
phenomena, 35
  perfection of, 39
philosophy, 58
physical exercise, 51
pitfalls, 21, 51
pleasure, 50, 51, 77
practice, 61, 66
pratyekabuddhas, 82. *See also* independent. . . .
preaching and listening, those who are
  content with, 72
presence, 32
  naked state of, 36
pride, 26, 41, 42
pride of transfiguration, 69

primordial freedom, 28, 47
primordial purity, 76
primordial yoga, 5, 50
principles, four, 3
pristine awareness, 14, 28, 29, 32, 42
  play of, 49
  self-generating, 36
  self-refreshing, 44
progress, 59, 61
  gradual, 46
projection, 62, 63, 64
provisional teachings, 20
psychic energies, 62
psycho-physical forces, 13
psychology, 58
psychotherapy, 59, 60
pure and total presence, 14, 33, 39,
    45, 47, 54, 73
  activity of, 40
  direct experience of, 1
  expand, 1
  stabilization in, 1
  state of, 1, 2, 32, 35, 37, 38, 39,
    78
pure experience, 43
pure fact of being, 28, 35, 36
pure presence, 40, 52, 72, 75
  and openness, unity of, 42
purification, 75

radiance, 76
Rang'-byung rdo-rje, 13
rBa rgyal-ba'i dbang-po, 28
rdzogs chen. See dzogchen.
rdzogs pa spyi gcod, 81
reality
  external, 14
  hidden dimension of, 83
  supreme, 6, 7
  unconditioned, 50
reality-field, 40, 41
realization, 15
  six levels of, 48
refinement, 75
  stages of, 4

reflections, 76
refuge, 29
relative condition, 59, 60
release, 37
religions, unity of, 58
renunciation, 69, 75
    path of, 4, 66 ff., 69
responsiveness, 75, 76
result, 8, 47 ff., 51. *See also* goal.
revolutions, three, 20, 21
richness of being, dimension of, 5, 7,
    20, 27, 28, 30, 38, 47
rig pa'i ku byug, 81
rMa Rin-chen mchog, 83
rmad byung, 82
rnying ma'i rgyud 'bum, 28, 83
    mTsham-brag edition, 83
    sDe-dge edition, 83
root tantra, 2, 3
rtsal chen yang dag drug pa, 81

sages, six, 31
Śākyamuni. *See* Buddha.
Samantabhadra, 20
sambhōgakāya, 4, 5, 27, 70. *See also*
    richness of being.
sameness, 38
samsara, 14, 15, 31, 32, 33, 50, 54,
    55, 75, 76
Sang-rgyas ye-shes, 82
sangs rgyas (Buddha), 76
sattvavajra, 7
self, 74
    -arising, 28
    -authentication, 27
    -confidence, 25
    -development, 19, 57
    -improvement, 59
    -knowledge, 57
    -mastery, 65
    -originating clear light, 36
    -origination, 39
self-liberation, 42, 69, 72, 77
    path of, 65, 66, 69
selfless, 34

selflessness, 29, 61
sems, 2, 74
sems dpa' rdo rje, 7
sems phyogs, 28
sems sde, 2, 80, 81, 82
sense, 52
    awareness, 14
    organs, 48
    perceptions, 49
    pleasure, 40
sentient beings, 32, 35, 37, 73
sex, 41, 60
sgom don drug pa, 81
sgra thal 'gyur, 3
sgyu, 2
sgyu 'phrul, 28
sgyu 'phrul drwa ba gsang ba'i snying po,
    2, 82
sheer presence, 51, 71
sku la 'jug pa, 81
sLob-dpon gzhon-nu don-grub, 28
sMin-gling gter-chen 'Gyur-med rdo-
    rje, 83
sNubs Sangs-rgyas ye-shes, 83
sNyags Jñānakumāra, 83
sNyan rin-chen rtse-mo, 28
snying thig, 82
Sog zlog-pa blo-gros rgyal-mtshan, 79
solar fire, 71
soul, 21
sound, 44
spiritual advisor, 24
spiritual guide, 51
spiritual pursuits, 22. *See also*
    approach.
spirituality, 54
spontaneously perfect inner reality, 44
spontaneously present, 76
śrāvakas, 82. *See also* listening and
    preaching. . . .
    Śrī Siṃha, 13, 28
    Śrī Saṃhaprabha, 84. *See also* Śrī
        Siṃha.
    srid pa'i rgyud, 81

stages to cultivate, 35
stages, two, 3, 4, 5, 69
striving, 37, 46, 51, 61
student, 25, 63, 64
stupidity, 40, 42
subtle reality, 35
supreme ordering principle, 1, 7, 27, 28, 39, 43, 72, 73
sutra, 4, 5, 6
sutric teaching, 64

tantra, 2, 4, 5, 6, 13, 64, 67, 70
   appended, 2
   branch, 2
   essential aspects of, 2, 3, 4, 34, 35
   explanatory, 2
   inner, 5
   root, 2, 3
tantrics, 42, 72
teacher, 37, 38, 43, 63, 64, 65, 74. *See also* guru, master.
   according to tantra, 67
teachers, five, 39. *See also* buddhas, five.
Theism, 73
thought, 37, 42, 44, 51, 60
   as play of energy, 68
   conceptual, 68
thought process, 14, 37
three realms, 45, 73
   beings of, 38, 39
three times, 73
Tilopa, 80
time, 74
total completeness, 21, 29, 49, 58, 71, 72
   primordial state of, 5
tradition, spiritual, 58
transcendent practices, six or ten, 21
transference, 62, 65
transformation, 4, 21, 69, 70, 75
   path of, 4, 5, 66, 69
   special methods of, 67
transmission, 62, 63

truth(s), 44
   conventional, 66
   two, 33
   ultimate, 66
tshad med bzhi bsgom, 70

Uḍḍiyāna, 28
ugliness, 44
unborn reality, 35, 36, 43, 45
uncontrived sameness, 36
universal creativity, 14, 19, 57
upadeśa, 6
utter sameness, 35
Vairocana rgyud 'bum, 7, 86
Vairocana, buddha, 5
Vairocana, translator, 7, 13, 28, 55, 81, 82, 84
vajra breathing, 31
vajradhara, unitary state of, 3, 4
vehicles, 23
Vimalamitra, 81, 82
Virupa, 80
vision, 14. *See also* perspective.
visualization, 13, 29 ff., 67, 68, 70
voice, 4, 67
   according to path of renunciation, 68
   according to path of transformation, 68
   as mantra, 68
void, 76. *See also* openness.

way of life, 40 ff., 46, 50, 52
wholeness, 62, 63, 64
wisdom
   accumulation of, 60
   transcendent, 21
worldly concerns, 24, 31

ye shes gsang ba, 81, 82
ye shes tshogs stong nyid bsgom, 70
yoga, 6
yogatantra, 3

Zur 'ug-pa, 83
Zur-ston rin-chen grags-pa, 28